the forefront of modern playwriting and some of the
most exciting developments in modern drama since 1959. To
commemorate the fiftieth anniversary of Methuen Drama, the
series was relaunched in 2009 as Methuen Drama Modern
Classics, and continues to offer readers a choice selection of the
best modern plays.

Accidental Death of an Anarchist

Written in 1970, *Morte accidentale di un'anarchico* is Dario Fo's
best-known and most popular play. In the first four years of its
production it was seen by an estimated one million people. A
sharp and hilarious satire on police corruption, and based on a
real case, Fo tells the story of the anarchist railway worker who,
in 1969, 'fell' to his death from a police headquarters window.
It is a piece in which his skill at writing farce and his gifts as a
clown brilliantly serve his politics, playing on the tensions
between the death of the prisoner and the farcical interventions
of the authorities to explain it.

Dario Fo was born in 1926 in Lombardy. He began working in
the theatre in 1951 as a comic and mime. Together with his wife,
Franca Rame, he was highly successful as actor, director and
writer of satirical comedies for the conventional theatre. In the
sixties they abandoned it; Fo began to write for a wider audience
in factories and workers' clubs and produced work which was not
only an important political intervention in Italy at the time but
has since become internationally acclaimed. In 1970 he and his
wife founded the theatrical collective La Comune in Milan. His
work – and the work of Franca Rame – has been performed in
England with great success: *Can't Pay? Won't Pay!* (Half Moon
Theatre and Criterion Theatre, London, 1981); *Accidental Death
of an Anarchist* (Half Moon Theatre and Wyndham's Theatre,
London, 1980); *Female Parts* by Franca Rame (National Theatre,
London, 1981); *Mistero Buffo* (Riverside Theatre, London, 1983);
Trumpets and Raspberries (Palace Theatre, Watford; Phoenix
Theatre, London, 1984); *Archangels Don't Play Pinball* (Bristol Old
Vic, 1986); *Elizabeth* (Half Moon Theatre, London, 1986); *An
Ordinary Day* (Borderline Theatre Company, Scotland, touring,
1988); and ... Playhouse,
Leeds, 1991 ... *Ordinary Day*
has also bee ... *Other*.

by the same author and also available from Bloomsbury Methuen Drama

Fo Plays: One
(Mistero Buffo, Accidental Death of an Anarchist, Trumpets
and Raspberries, The Virtuous Burglar, One Was Nude and
One Wore Tails)

Fo Plays: Two
(Can't Pay? Won't Pay!, Elizabeth, The Open Couple, An
Ordinary Day)

Tricks of the Trade

My First Seven Years (plus a few more)

by Dario Fo and Franca Rame

A Woman Alone and other plays

DARIO FO

Accidental Death of an Anarchist

Adapted by Gavin Richards
from a translation by Gillian Hanna

Introduced by Stuart Hood

Bloomsbury Methuen Drama
An imprint of Bloomsbury Publishing Plc

B L O O M S B U R Y
LONDON · OXFORD · NEW YORK · NEW DELHI · SYDNEY

Bloomsbury Methuen Drama

An imprint of Bloomsbury Publishing Plc

Imprint previously known as Methuen Drama

50 Bedford Square	1385 Broadway
London	New York
WC1B 3DP	NY 10018
UK	USA

www.bloomsbury.com

BLOOMSBURY, METHUEN DRAMA and the Diana logo are trademarks of Bloomsbury Publishing Plc

First published in Great Britain by Pluto Press Ltd, 1980
Corrected edition with Stuart Hood's introduction first published in Great Britain by Methuen Drama, 1987
This edition, with new cover design, published in 2001 by Methuen Publishing Limited
Reissued with a new cover design by Bloomsbury Methuen Drama 2009
Reprinted 2014, 2015 (twice)

British Library Cataloguing-in-Publication Data
A catalogue record for this book is available from the British Library.

ISBN: PB: 978-0-4131-5610-5

Library of Congress Cataloging-in-Publication Data
A catalog record for this book is available from the Library of Congress.

Series: Modern Classics

Printed and bound in India

Contents

INTRODUCTION
The Theatre of Dario Fo and Franca Rame

The son of a railway worker, Dario Fo was born in 1926 near the Lago Maggiore in Northern Italy. He grew up in a village community that included glass-blowers and smugglers, where there was a strong tradition of popular narrative – much of it humorously subversive of authority – fed by travelling story-tellers and puppeteers. Gifted artistically, he studied architecture at Milan at the art-school attached to the Brera Gallery; but the theatre drew him strongly – first as a set-designer and then as a performer. His career began in revue which was the spectacular escapist entertainment of post-war Italy with girls and comics (some very brilliant like Totò, whom Fo greatly admired) and glamorous *chanteuses*. It was a genre favoured by politicians of the ruling Christian Democrat party; girls' legs were preferable to the social preoccupations of contemporary Italian cinema. In revue Fo began to make his mark as an extraordinarily original comic and mime. On radio he built a reputation with his monologues as a Poer Nano – the poor simpleton who, in telling Bible stories, for example, gets things wrong, preferring Cain to the insufferable prig, Abel. In 1954 he married Franca Rame, a striking and talented actress, who came from a family of travelling players and had made her first stage appearance when she was eight days old. Together they embarked on a highly successful series of productions.

In the fifties the right-wing clerical Christian Democrat government had imposed a tight censorship on film, theatre and broadcasting. Fo took advantage of a slight relaxation in censorship to mount an 'anti-revue', *Il dito nell'occhio* (One in the Eye). His aim was clear – to attack those myths in Italian life which, as he said, 'Fascism had imposed and Christian Democracy had preserved.' *Il dito nell'occhio* was 'one in the eye' for official versions of history. Presented at the Piccolo Teatro in Milan it was an immense success to which the participation of the great French mime, Jacques Lecoq, from whom Fo learned much, was an important contribution. *Il dito nell'occhio* was the first in a series of pieces which drew on French farce, on the traditional sketches of the Rame family, and on the traditions of the circus. This mixture of spectacle, mime and social comment was highly successful but made the authorities nervous; the police were frequently present at performances, following the scripts with pocket torches to ensure that there were no departures from the officially approved text. Fo grew in stature and virtuosity as actor and comic, exploiting his extraordinary range of gesture, movement and facial expression, his variety of voices and accents, and his skill as a story-teller. It was the misfortune of Italian cinema that it was unable to exploit his talents. There were difficulties in finding suitable scripts and, on set, his vitality and spontaneity were denied the space and freedom that the theatre provided. But what Fo did take away from film was an understanding of how montage gave pace to narrative.

In 1959 the Dario Fo–Franca Rame company was invited to open a season at the Odeon Theatre in Milan. The piece they chose was *Gli arcangeli non giocano a flipper* (Archangels Don't Play Pinball), written, directed and designed by Fo. It was unusual in that it dealt critically with certain ludicrous aspects of Italian society. The middle-class audience were astonished by its rhythms and technique and delighted by Fo in the leading role – that of a wise simpleton, who looks back to Poer Nano and forward to a series of similar clowns in later work. Fo and Rame were now securely established both as actors and as personalities in the public eye. Their success in conventional theatre was confirmed by a series of pieces which exploited a mixture of comedy, music and farcical plots in which Fo would, for instance, double as an absent-minded priest and a bandit. The social references were there – Fo and Rame were now both close to the Communist Party and acutely aware of the political tensions in society – and the public readily picked them up. In a period which saw widespread industrial unrest culminating in the general strike of 1960 their material caused the authorities in Milan to threaten to ban performances.

Italian television had been for many years a fief of the Christian Democrats. Programme control was strict: a young woman given to wearing tight sweaters who looked like winning a popular quiz show had to be eliminated on moral grounds. But when in 1962 the centre-left of the Christian Democrats became dominant there was some relaxation of censorship. It was in these circumstances that the Fo–Rame team was invited to appear on the most popular TV show, *Canzonissima*, which, as its name suggests, featured heart-throb singers along with variety acts. Into this show the Fo's proceeded to inject their own brand of subversive humour – such as a sketch in which a worker whose aunt has fallen into a mincing-machine, which cannot be stopped for that would interrupt production, piously takes her home as tinned meat. The reaction of the political authorities and of the right-wing press was to call for censorship, duly imposed by the obedient functionaries of Italian television – all of them political appointees. There was a tussle of wills at the end of which the Fo's walked out of the show. The scandal was immense. There were parliamentary questions; threats of law-suits on both sides. Fo had public opinion solidly behind him. He had, he said, tried to look behind the facade of the 'economic miracle', to question the view that 'we were all one big family now' and to show how exploitation had increased and scandals flourished. By subverting *Canzonissima* from within he had established himself with a huge popular audience.

During this period Fo had become interested in material set in or drawn from the Middle Ages. He had begun 'to look at the present with the instruments of history and culture in order to judge it better'. He invited the public to use these instruments by writing an ambitious piece, *Isabella, tre*

caravelle e un cacciaballe (Isabella, Three Caravels and a
Wild-Goose Chaser), in which Columbus – that schoolbook
hero – is portrayed as the upwards striving intellectual who
loses out in the game of high politics. It was a period when
Brecht's *Galileo* was playing with great success in Milan and
the theatre was a subject of intense debate in the intellectual
and political ferment leading up to the unrest of 1968. For Fo
the most important result was probably his collaboration with
a group of left-wing musicians who had become interested in
the political potential of popular songs. Their work appealed
to him because he was himself 'interested above all in a past
attached to the roots of the people... and the concept of "the
new in the traditional".' They put together a show, built
round popular and radical songs, to which Fo contributed his
theories on the importance of gesture and the rhythms in the
performance of folksong; it marked an important step in his
development.

In 1967 he put on his last production for the bourgeois
theatre, *La signora non è da buttare* (The Lady's Not For
Discarding), in which a circus was made the vehicle for an
attack on the United States and capitalist society in general. It
again attracted the attention of the authorities. Fo was called
to police headquarters in Milan and threatened with arrest for
'offensive lines', not included in the approved version,
attacking a head of state – Lyndon Johnson. By now it was
becoming 'more and more difficult to act in a theatre where
everything down to the subdivision of the seating... mirrored
the class divisions. The choice for an intellectual', Fo
concluded, 'was to leave his gilded ghetto and put himself at
the disposal of the movement.'

The company with which the Fo's confronted this task was
the cooperative Nuova Scena – an attempt to dispense with
the traditional roles in a stage company and to make
decision-making collective. It was, Fo said in retrospect, a
utopian project in which individual talents and capabilities
were sacrificed to egalitarian principles. But whatever the
internal difficulties there was no doubt as to the success the
company enjoyed with a new public which it sought out in the
working-class estates, in cooperatives and trade union halls,

in factories and workers' clubs. It was a public which knew nothing of the theatre but which found the political attitudes the company presented close to its experience of life. Each performance was followed by a discussion.

Nuova Scena did not last long – it was torn apart by political arguments, by arguments over the relationship of art to society and politics, and by questions of organisation. There were also difficulties with the Communist Party, which often controlled the premises used and whose officials began to react negatively to satirical attacks on their bureaucracy, the inflexibility of the Party line, the intolerance of real discussion. Before the split came, the company had put on a *Grande pantomima con bandiere e pupazzi medi e piccoli* (Grand Pantomime with Flags and Little and Medium Puppets), in which Fo used a huge puppet, drawn from the Sicilian tradition, to represent the state and its continual fight with the 'dragon' of the working class. But the most important production was Fo's one-man show *Mistero Buffo*, which was to become one of his enduring triumphs in Italy and abroad. In it he drew on the counter-culture of the Middle Ages, on apocryphal gospel stories, on legend and tales, presenting episodes in which he played all the roles and used a language in part invented, in part archaic, in part drawn from the dialects of Northern Italy. It has been described as 'an imaginary Esperanto of the poor and disinherited'. In performing the scenes of which *Mistero Buffo* is composed – such as the resurrection of Lazarus, the marriage at Cana, Pope Boniface's encounter with Jesus on the Via Dolorosa and others – Fo drew on two main traditions: that of the *giullare* (inadequately translated into English as 'jester'), the travelling comic, singer, mime, who in the Middle Ages was the carrier of a subversive culture; and that of the great clowns of the Commedia dell'Arte with their use of masks, of dialect and of *grammelot*, that extraordinary onomatopoeic rendering of a language – French, say – invented by the 15th-century comedians in which there are accurate sounds and intonations but few real words, all adding up (with the aid of highly expressive mime) to intelligible discourse.

When Nuova Scena split in 1970 it came hard on the heels of mounting polemics in the Communist press. Looking back, Franca Rame has admitted that she and Dario Fo were perhaps sectarian and sometimes mistaken but that they had had to break with the Communist cultural organisations if they wished to progress. The result was La Comune, a theatre company with its headquarters in Milan. The Fo's were now politically linked to the new Left, which found the Communist Party too authoritarian, too locked in the mythology of the Resistance, too inflexible and increasingly conservative. In *Morte accidentale di un'anarchico* (Accidental Death of an Anarchist) Fo produced a piece in which his skill at writing farce and his gifts as a clown were put brilliantly at the service of his politics, playing on the tension between the real death of a prisoner and the farcical inventions advanced by the authorities to explain it. It is estimated that in four years the piece was seen by a million people, many of whom took part in fierce debates after the performance. Fo had succeeded in his aim of making of the theatre 'a great machine which makes people laugh at dramatic things... In the laughter there remains a sediment of anger.' So no easy catharsis. There followed a period in which Fo was deeply engaged politically – both through his writings and through his involvement with Franca Rame, who was the main mover of the project – in Red Aid, which collected funds and comforts for Italian political prisoners detained in harsh conditions. His writing dealt with the Palestinian struggle, with Chile, with the methods of the Italian police. In the spring of 1973 Franca Rame was kidnapped from her home in Milan by a Fascist gang, gravely assaulted and left bleeding in the street. Fo himself later that year was arrested and held in prison in Sardinia for refusing to allow police to be present at rehearsals. Demonstrations and protests ensured his release. Dario Fo had, as his lawyer said, for years no longer been only an actor but a political figure whom the state powers would use any weapon to silence.

His political flair was evident in the farce *Non si paga, non si paga* (Can't Pay? Won't Pay!) dating from 1974, which deals with the question of civil disobedience. Significantly, the main upholder of law and order is a Communist shop steward, who disapproves of his wife's gesture of rebellion against the rising cost of living – a raid on a supermarket. It was a piece tried out on and altered at the suggestion of popular audiences – a practice Fo has often used. It was the same spirit that inspired his *Storia di una tigre* (Story of a Tiger), an allegorical monologue dating from 1980 – after a trip to China, and based on a Chinese folktale – the moral of which is that, if you have 'tiger' in you, you must never delegate responsibility to others, never expect others to solve your own problems, and above all avoid that unthinking party loyalty which is the enemy of reason and of revolution. In 1981, following on the kidnapping of Aldo Moro came *Clacson, trombette e pernacchi* (Trumpets and Raspberries). In it Fo doubled as Agnelli, the boss of FIAT, and a FIAT shop steward, whose identities become farcically confused. The play mocks the police and their readiness to see terrorists everywhere and the political cynicism which led to Moro's being abandoned to his fate by his fellow-politicians.

It was the last of Fo's major political works to date. Looking for new fields at a time when the great political upsurge has died away and the consumerist state has apparently triumphed, Fo has turned in recent years to a play on Elizabeth and Essex, with a splendid transvestite part for himself which allows him to use the dialect of *Mistero Buffo*, and a Harlequinade – a slight but charming piece that returns to the techniques of the Commedia dell'Arte.

Meanwhile Franca Rame, who has progressively established herself as a political figure and a powerful feminist, has produced a number of one-woman plays, partly in collaboration with her husband – monologues which are a direct political intervention in a society where the role of women is notably restricted by the Church, the state and male traditions. Like all their work the one-woman plays such as *Il risveglio* (Waking Up) or *Una donna sola* (A Woman Alone) depend on the tension between the unbearable nature of the situation in which the female protagonist finds herself and the grotesque behaviour of people around her – in particular the men. It is a theme which is treated with anger and disgust in

Lo stupro (The Rape), tragically in her version of *Medea* and comically in *Coppia aperta* (Open Couple) in which the hypocrisies of 'sexual liberation' are dissected.

Dario Fo and Franca Rame have a world-wide reputation. The Scandinavian countries were among the first to welcome them as performers and to produce their work. The whole of Western Europe has by now acknowledged their importance and virtuosity. Ironically the Berliner Ensemble, the theatre founded by Brecht to whom Fo owes so much, found Fo's rock version of *The Beggar's Opera* too difficult to take in spite of Brecht's advice to treat famous authors with disrespect if you have the least consideration for the ideas they express. It had to be staged in Italy. Foreign travel has not been without its problems: attacks on the theatre where they played in Buenos Aires under military rule and a visa to the United States long refused. The summer of 1986 saw the American administration at last relent, which may be some sort of comment on how they judge the Fo's impact and importance in the present political climate.

STUART HOOD
September 1986

Author's Note

A few days before Christmas eleven years ago – on 12 December 1969 – a bomb exploded in the Agricultural Bank in Milan. It was a massacre – more than 16 dead. The anarchists were immediately blamed for the slaughter. One of them, Giovanni Pinelli, having been taken to police headquarters, flew out of the window on the fourth floor. The police declared that Pinelli had committed suicide after having been convinced that the real culprits were no other than Valpreda, Garganelli, and the other members of the Milan group.

Ten years later, at Catanzaro in Southern Italy, the trial resulting from the slaughter in Milan came to an end. Three fascists were condemned to prison for being materially responsible for the crime. One of them, Giannettini, turned out to be an agent for the Italian secret police; it was thus confirmed beyond all doubt that the instigators of the crime had been the organisations entrusted with the 'protection' of the Italian state. The instigators, as was clear from the sentence of the court, were to be found among the upper ranks of the military and political institutions. Ministers and generals were brought into court – but it all ended, as usual, in a great smoke-screen. Generals and ministers were first condemned and then acquitted. It was only the criminal 'labour force' that went to prison.

Today, at the beginning of the 1980s, things are clearer. But when the play was first staged in Milan, in the shed of an old factory transformed into a theatre – the Capannone of Via Colletta – the view of almost the entire population, thanks to the 'magnificent' information work carried out by the national and international media, was that the massacre was to be attributed to subversive groups of the extreme left.

Our intervention, as the La Comune collective, was therefore, above all, an exercise in counterinformation. Using authentic documents – and complete transcripts of the investigations carried out by the various judges as well as police reports – we turned the logic and the truth of the facts on head. But the great and provocative impact of this play was determined by its theatrical form: rooted in tragedy, the play became farce – the farce of power. The public who came to the theatre – progressive students, workers, but also large numbers of the lower middle classes – was overwhelmed by the grotesque and apparently mad way in which the play worked. They split their sides laughing at the effects produced by the comical and at the same time satirical situations. But as the performance went on, they gradually came to see that they were laughing the whole time at real events, events which were criminal and obscene in their brutality: crimes of the state.

So the grins froze on their faces and in most cases turned into a kind of *Grand Guignol* scream which had nothing liberating about it, nothing to make things palatable – on the contrary, it made them impossible to swallow.

Pinelli, or rather his corpse and with it the 16 corpses of the massacre, were a constant presence on the stage. This was something the public commented on during the discussions at the end of each performance.

The tragic farce of *Accidental Death* was repeated all over Italy for more than two years on end. It was seen by more than half a million people and it was published in three different editions. Why three different editions? Simply because the play had to follow the increased consciousness of Italian public opinion and the sharpening struggle by the working class and the student movement, and to evolve the political developments that resulted from absorbing themes and syntheses from the new political and social events which were emerging.

In the daily debates which took place after performances it was the public itself which jogged us towards greater clarity about the new struggles which were growing daily and developing throughout the country.

It is obvious that the theatrical theme and, above all, the enormous success which it enjoyed, produced a violent reaction in the centres of power. So we were subjected to provocation and persecution of all kinds, sometimes more grotesque and comical in their repressive stupidity than the very farce which we were performing. The English public, seeing this play in its present adaptation, obviously cannot feel the real, tragic, tangible atmosphere which the Italian public brought with them when they came to the performance. It can share this only by the act of imagination or – better still – by substituting for the violence practised by the powers in Italy (the police, the judiciary, the economy of the banks and the multinationals) equally tragic and brutal facts from the recent history of England.

I am aware, in connection with the adaptation which follows, that certain moments in the play which were of obvious theatrical and political importance at the time had necessarily to be replaced because of their limited reference – that is to say, because an English audience would be unaware of their background and, above all, because it is impossible to restate them in a theatrical context with sufficient pithiness and immediacy.

So I have the impression – more than an impression – that some passages which have been skipped in Gavin Richards' version may have produced some erosion at a satirical level, that is to say in the relationship of the tragic to the grotesque, which was the foundation of the original work, in favour of solutions which are exclusively comic. But it is also true that, because of a particular historical and cultural process, the taste for satire touches a very deeply rooted feeling in the Italian public – amongst the working class as well as the middle classes, and even the sub-proletariat.

The taste for satire was not suppressed even by fascism – in fact it developed. By good fortune our Italian bourgeoisie has always shown itself to be more stupid than its counterparts in the rest of Europe. It didn't devote as much effort to destroying the cultural forms peculiar to the lower classes and to replacing their traditions, their rituals, their language – in short their 'vulgar' powers of expression and creativity – with the ruthlessness and thoroughness used by the French, German and English bourgeoisie. Perhaps it wasn't able to.

We Italians 'enjoyed' the industrial revolution after a long time-lag. So we are not yet a sufficiently modern nation to have forgotten the ancient feeling for satire. That is why we can still laugh, with a degree of cynicism, at the macabre dance which power and the civilisation that goes with it performs daily, without waiting for carnival.

An old Sicilian song goes:

A woman crossing the square slips in the mud
and falls head over heels.
Her skirts go over her head
She shows her bum
The fools laugh fit to burst and shout dirty words
The King passes on horseback, the mud makes him slip
The fine beast and the King roll on the ground
and in his turn he shows his bum through his torn breeches.
The fools rush to take off their hats
Only a madman across the way
seeing this new and unfamiliar face of power
can't help laughing his head off.

The fools chorus at the top of their voices –
so as to drown the madman's laughter –
their praise of the great royal bum
'Oh, magnificent cheeks basking in the sun
hailed by God, wonderful spheres'
The fools, because the King has shit himself, for fear,
begin to praise the stink of the noble motion
The madman runs up waving a censer
and sings *Te Deum* to the King's shit
and plants a jasmine sprig in it.
The fools applaud and then by a miracle understand the jape
and take up stones and sticks
and make to lynch the mocker.
But since they know it is great bad luck
to kill a madman

protected as they are by the pity of St Francis
'the great madman of God'
the fools, impotently watch the pantomime of the madman.
Later at home, in secret, each one by himself
remembers the madman's pantomime and laughs.
They laugh till they pee themselves.
The fools for a moment forget they are
fools but only for a moment
because, alas, madmen are few and far between
and the fools don't get much chance
to see their mad, obscene pantomimes.

From the collection researched by Giovanni Pitré (19th century)

DARIO FO, 1980

The translation by Gillian Hanna and this adaptation was originally commissioned and subsequently presented on tour by Belt & Braces Roadshow Company. The first performance was at Dartington College in January 1979 and the cast was as follows:

MANIAC	Fred Molina
BERTOZZO	Terence John
PISSANI	Robert Macintosh
CONSTABLES	Stephen Coke
SUPERINTENDENT	Andrew De La Tour
FELETTI	Eileen Pollock

The same production subsequently transferred to the Half Moon Theatre, London, and then to Wyndhams Theatre, London, where it opened 5 March 1980. The cast was as follows:

MANIAC	Gavin Richards
BERTOZZO	Jim Bywater
PISSANI	Ken Gregson
SUPERINTENDENT	John Gillet
CONSTABLES	Gavin Muir
FELETTI	Jeni Barnett

Act One
Scene One

An ordinary office in the Central Police HQ, Milan. A desk littered with papers and files, telephone and card listing extensions, a bench, chairs, filing cabinet, a wastepaper bin, and a coat stand on which hang various coats and hats. The room is drab and bureaucratic; it is dominated by a large window. There are two doors. The view from the window indicates the office to be on the first floor. Enter INSPECTOR BERTOZZO *and a* CONSTABLE *who takes the Inspector's coat and hat to the coat stand.*

BERTOZZO: (*To Audience*) Good evening. I am Inspector Francesco Giovanni Batista Giancarlo Bertozzo of the Security Police. This is my office on the first floor of our notorious headquarters here in Milan. Notorious following a sordid little incident a few weeks ago when an anarchist, under interrogation in a similar room a few floors above, fell through the window. Although my colleagues claimed, quite reasonably, that the incident was suicide, the official verdict of the enquiry is that the death of the anarchist was 'accidental'. Bit ambiguous you see. So there's been public outrage, accusations, demonstrations and so on flying around this building for weeks. Not the best atmosphere in which a decent nine to five plainclothes policeman like myself can do an honest inconspicuous day's work.

I get all types in here. Tea leaves, junkies, pimps, arsonists – this is a sort of clearing house. NEXT!

Exit CONSTABLE. *Returns with the character known as* 'MANIAC' *who sits opposite the desk. He looks like the cliché idea of a disciple of Freud: wild hair, thin spectacles, goatee beard, shabby suit or mac. He sits calmly. He carries about four plastic carrier bags stuffed with god knows what.*

BERTOZZO: I ought to warn you that the author of this sick little play, Dario Fo, has the traditional, irrational hatred of the police common to all narrow-minded left-wingers and so I shall, no doubt, be the unwilling butt of endless anti-authoritarian jibes.

CONSTABLE *encounters a mouse trap hidden in the filing cabinet and he yells.*

BERTOZZO: Please bear with me.

INSPECTOR BERTOZZO *picks up a visiting card and studies it, looking up at the* MANIAC.

BERTOZZO: This isn't the first time that you've been up for impersonation is it? In all you have been arrested... let me see...

He leafs through the papers in front of him.

BERTOZZO: Twice as a surgeon, three times as a bishop, army captain, tennis umpire...

MANIAC: Eleven arrests altogether, but I'd like to point out that I have never actually been convicted, Inspector.

BERTOZZO: I don't know how the hell you have been getting away with it, but this time we'll have you. That's a promise.

MANIAC: Mouthwatering, isn't it? A nice clean record like mine just begging to be defiled.

BERTOZZO: The charges state that you falsely assumed the identity of a professor of psychiatry and former don of the University of Padua. That's fraud.

MANIAC: Fraud when committed by a sane man, yes indeed, but I am a lunatic. A certified psychotic! There's my medical report.

He hands BERTOZZO *a crumpled piece of paper.*

MANIAC: Committed sixteen times, same thing every time –

'Histrionic mania' from the Latin, *histriones*, 'to act the part of' – my hobby, you see, the theatre; and my theatre is the theatre of reality so my fellow artistes must be real people, unaware that they are acting in my productions, which is handy, as you see, I've got no cash to pay them.

BERTOZZO: Exactly, you swindle them.

MANIAC: I have never swindled anyone.

CONSTABLE: Not much.

MANIAC: I applied for a grant from the Ministry of Culture but I hadn't got the right connections.

BERTOZZO: According to my notes, as this psychiatrist you were charging your clients two hundred thousand lire a visit.

CONSTABLE: Jesus wept!

MANIAC: I beg your pardon?

CONSTABLE: I could retire on that.

MANIAC: It's a reasonable fee for a man with my qualifications.

BERTOZZO: What qualifications?

MANIAC: Twenty years of intensive training in sixteen different loony bins under some of the best shrinks in the biz. Unlike your run-of-the-mill man I immersed myself in my studies, slept with them as well when the beds ran out – head to toe, three in a kip, make your own enquiries, I am a bloody genius! Look at my brilliant diagnosis of that millionaire's schizophrenic son in Palermo. Superb!

BERTOZZO: Superb fee, OK.

MANIAC: The fee is an indispensable part of the treatment. If I didn't relieve these twits of the odd two hundred thousand I'd lose all credibility. Any less and they'd think I was no good, a beginner or something. Even Freud… Ah, Sigmund (*He crosses himself*) …even Freud said a fat bill is the most effective panacea especially for the doctor.

BERTOZZO: Pity your client filed a complaint, wasn't it.

He holds up a visiting card.

BERTOZZO: This is your visiting card, is it not?

MANIAC: It is.

BERTOZZO: (*Reading*) 'Professor Antonio Rabbia, Psychiatrist. Formerly, lecturer at the University of Padua'. Are you Antonio Rabbia?

MANIAC: Not exactly.

BERTOZZO: What's that mean?

MANIAC: I am a professor.

BERTOZZO: You are, eh?

MANIAC: Yes. Of design, decoration and freehand drawing at the College of the Sacred Redeemer. I take evening classes.

BERTOZZO: It says here, psychiatrist.

MANIAC: After the comma?

BERTOZZO: Yes.

MANIAC: Before the full stop?

BERTOZZO: Yes.

MANIAC: Exactly.

BERTOZZO: Exactly what?

MANIAC: 'Professor Antonio Rabbia' comma, capital 'P' – 'Psychiatrist' full stop. I take it you are familiar with the basic rules of syntax and punctuation. Where's the fraud?

CONSTABLE: Definitely a crackpot, sir.

BERTOZZO: 'Formerly, lecturer at the University of Padua.' True or false?

MANIAC: After the 'formerly'…?

BERTOZZO: What?

MANIAC: Another comma. Can't you even read?

BERTOZZO: I hadn't noticed it.

MANIAC: You don't notice these things and innocent people like me are thrown behind bars.

BERTOZZO: You are mad.

MANIAC: I know.

BERTOZZO: What have these commas got to do with it?

MANIAC: Nothing to someone with your rudimentary education evidently. Look... a minute... the punctuation changes the whole emphasis of the sentence. After the comma, the reader – your good self – takes a short mental breath thus changing the intentionality. You see? So, the sentence should read... 'Professor Antonio Rabbia' ...comma ...capital 'P' 'Psychiatrist!!!' Full stop... 'Formerly'... comma... 'Lecturer at the University of Padua!!!' You see, read correctly only an arsehole would swallow it.

BERTOZZO: I'm an arsehole am I?!

MANIAC: No! No! Your grammar is a bit retarded, that's all. I could give you a refresher course. Cut rate, naturally. Haven't done too well out of this year's spending cuts have you boys? Let's begin by repeating all subjective and objective, in Italian, pronouns beginning thus... *io sono, tu sei, loro sono, lei...*

Launches off into Italian at CONSTABLE.

MANIAC: Eh... eh...

CONSTABLE: ...Eh...

MANIAC: Good. (*To* BERTOZZO) You too, Franco, no shirking.

BERTOZZO: May we... !!

MANIAC: ...That's French...

BERTOZZO: (*Thumping the desk*) MAY WE GET ON WITH THIS FUCKING STATEMENT!

MANIAC: Fine. I'll type. Qualified secretary, forty-five words a minute...

BERTOZZO: Shut up!

MANIAC: Shorthand? I am a Pitman's man myself... Where do you keep the carbon?

BERTOZZO: GET THE CUFFS ON HIM!

The CONSTABLE *takes out his handcuffs.* MANIAC *has a fit ending up with...*

MANIAC: Ah ah. Strait-jacket or nothing. Article 122 of the Penal Code states, 'Whoever in his capacity as a public official imposes non-clinical instruments of restraint upon a psychologically disturbed person in a manner liable to provoke a crisis in the disturbance shall incur charges punishable by five to fifteen years with forfeit of pension.'

CONSTABLE: Ah. (*He backs off, terrified of losing his pension*)

BERTOZZO: Law student as well now, eh?

MANIAC: (*Disdainfully*) Student?

BERTOZZO: Studied court procedure in the loony bin no doubt.

MANIAC: A paranoid registrar gave lectures three mornings a week: Roman Law, Modern Law, Ecclesiastical Law. Test me.

BERTOZZO: Don't be fooled, Constable. This raving is a conscious effort to confuse us and avoid prosecution.

MANIAC: No it's not...

BERTOZZO: Sit down!!

MANIAC *sits.*

BERTOZZO: So, a bit of a lawyer too, eh? Is this a clue to further undetected transgressions? Nothing in your curriculum vitae about a lawyer, not even a barrister here.

MANIAC: Who wants to be a barrister? I don't want to be passive. I don't want to defend. I'm like you, Inspector. I like to accuse, convict, judge and pass sentence.

BERTOZZO: Never actually impersonated a judge, have you? Just for the record?

MANIAC: Unfortunately the opportunity hasn't arisen so far.

CONSTABLE: Shame.

MANIAC: Yes, but oh I'd love to do a judge. You see the thing about judges is that they never retire. That's the beauty of it. Your ordinary humdrum sons and daughters of toil, they hit sixty and they're finished, they slow down, get sloppy, sluggish, whoops onto the scrap heap – at that very same moment that your average magistrate blooms into a high court judge…

BERTOZZO: Will you…

MANIAC: Silence in the court!!!

BERTOZZO: (*Caught off guard*) Beg your pardon M'Lud.

MANIAC: See what I mean. Take your lathe operator – touch of the shakes, couple of minor accidents, out to grass. Coal miner, bit of silicosis and he's fucked at fifty. Housewife, there's a job, she never retires either, but the older she grows the more she does the less she gets and she ends up with nothing. But the frailer and feebler judges get, the more they are elevated to superior and powerful positions. Oh yes, that's the job for me. 'Fifty years for you, thirty years for you. Case dismissed. Council can come and corrupt me in my chambers.'

CONSTABLE moves towards MANIAC *with handcuffs at the ready.*

MANIAC: Hands off or I'll bite!

CONSTABLE: What?

MANIAC: In the arse. Can't control it. GRrrrrr!

MANIAC *chases* CONSTABLE *round the room.*

CONSTABLE: I warned you, sir. He's crazy.

BERTOZZO: Grab him, Constable.

CONSTABLE: But he bites.

MANIAC: And I've got rabies. Caught it off a dog. Rabid bastard, took a lump out me right here…

CONSTABLE: (*Indicating right ear*) Right ear?

MANIAC: No. Right here.

Grabs at CONSTABLE.

MANIAC: Well he's dead and I'm cured... Cured but still contagious. Grrrr!

BERTOZZO: What are you, a lump of lard? Cuff him one.

CONSTABLE: (*Terrified*) He's bonkers I tell you.

BERTOZZO: Nonsense.

CONSTABLE: He's bananas.

MANIAC *is sniffing the floor like a dog. They creep up on him.*

BERTOZZO: Go for him!

They rush at MANIAC *and hit each other.* MANIAC *escapes to the window and opens it. Sits on the ledge.*

MANIAC: I'll throw myself out! How high are we? I will.

BERTOZZO: Bugger him! I'll give him a hand.

CONSTABLE: This place has got a bad enough record as it is. We can't afford another one.

BERTOZZO: You're right, Constable.

CONSTABLE: I know I'm right.

MANIAC: And when I'm down there all sludgy on the pavement and doing the death rattle – and be warned I shall take a long time to die and I'll be rattling a lot – the journalists will be flocking round and I'll tell them, rattling away, that you pushed me!! (*He makes to jump*)

BERTOZZO: Please stop it! Come down. We shan't harm you.

MANIAC: You won't rough me up?

BERTOZZO: I promise.

MANIAC: Remember the codicil to article 122 'Provocation and violence towards those of unsound mind...

ALL: ...six to nine years and loss of rank.'

MANIAC: You remembered.

CONSTABLE: Please.

CONSTABLE helps MANIAC from the window.

BERTOZZO: Lock the window.

As the CONSTABLE goes to shut the window, the MANIAC makes a bolt for the door.

MANIAC: I could always throw myself down the stairs!

BERTOZZO: Lock that bloody door.

MANIAC: Bumpety, bumpety, crack, splat, over the banisters.

BERTOZZO throws CONSTABLE the key. CONSTABLE locks the door.

BERTOZZO: And then throw the key...

MANIAC: Out of the window.

BERTOZZO: Yes.

CONSTABLE heads for the window.

BERTOZZO: No! Put it in the drawer. Open the drawer and put the key in the drawer...

CONSTABLE puts the key in the drawer.

BERTOZZO: And lock the drawer and...

MANIAC: Put the key in your mouth and swallow it.

BERTOZZO: Yes... !

CONSTABLE goes to swallow key.

BERTOZZO: No! That's it! I've had it! *I'm* raving now. *I've* gone blinding crazy now! Nobody has ever done this to me! Nobody!

He grabs the MANIAC .

BERTOZZO: You think you're potty?

MANIAC: Yes indeed!

BERTOZZO: I am much pottier!

MANIAC: Join the club.

BERTOZZO: (*To* CONSTABLE) OPEN THE DOOR!

CONSTABLE *unlocks drawer, takes out key and re-opens door.*

MANIAC: Let me stay.

BERTOZZO: Out!

MANIAC: I can help you.

BERTOZZO: Throw yourself down the stairs you fruitcake!

MANIAC: No need to be so rough.

MANIAC *struggles to gain possession of his plastic carrier bags lying in a heap by his chair.*

BERTOZZO: Put your fucking head under a bus.

MANIAC: I can help you make subversives talk.

BERTOZZO: Slash your wrists.

MANIAC: I can injure without visible signs.

BERTOZZO: Do what you like! I don't care!

MANIAC: I know how to make nitroglycerine suppositories!

BERTOZZO: OUT!!

CONSTABLE *and* BERTOZZO *fling him through the door. Followed by his carrier bags.*

BERTOZZO: At last! Thank God for that. I hope we never get another one like that. What time is it?

CONSTABLE: We're five minutes late for your meeting with Superintendent Bellati, sir.

BERTOZZO: Why didn't you tell me?

CONSTABLE: You were otherwise engaged.

BERTOZZO: Come on.

They leave by other door. Silence. A tap on the first door. Re-enter MANIAC *cautiously.*

MANIAC: Inspector? ...Please don't be angry with me again, I've just come back to collect my papers. Hello... Hello...

He sees the room is empty.

MANIAC: Oh... Inspector? Mnn.

He goes to the desk and picks up his file, opens it and checks the contents.

MANIAC: Medical record, prescription book, visiting card, charge sheet... What's this?

He notices other files on the desk. He flips over them.

MANIAC: Loitering with intent. Grand larceny.
Shopfitting... lifting... must get these glasses fixed.

Pokes his finger through glasses – no glass.

MANIAC: Car theft: subject apprehended after car chase with a steamroller. Good man.

He takes files to window.

MANIAC: Nobody move. Justice has arrived.

He empties files out of the window.

MANIAC: You're free, free, absolutely free! Not so free.

He opens top drawer of filing cabinet and looks through.

MANIAC: Oooh I see, the big fish. *Pesci grossi!* Diamond smugglers, drug racketeers. You can all stay there. Where are all the little people? I know.

Closes top drawer and opens bottom drawer. Looks through.

MANIAC: That's more like it. Heads!

Takes an armful of files and empties them out of the window.

MANIAC: Oh, sorry Padre.

The telephone rings. He answers it, taking it over and putting it on the filing cabinet so he can continue to dispense justice as he talks.

MANIAC: Hello, Inspector Bertozzo's office, whom do I

have the honour of addressing? ...No, no, you tell me who you are and I might hand you over to him... Who? ...Oh how delightful... (*Holding phone away*) ...Bertozzo, it's good old Inspector Defenestration himself... Our little joke... from the French *fenêtre* meaning window, i.e. 'defenestration', 'to chuck out from same'. Take it easy. Four!

Another file out of the window.

MANIAC: ...Office golf, Bertozzo's losing three under par. I'm the caddy.

Another file.

MANIAC: What do you mean? (*Holding phone away*) Here, Bertozzo! That old scourge of the ultra-left up there on the... er... fourth floor wants to know who I am. I may not be as famous as he is for chucking my cases out of windows, but I'm doing my best. Four!

Another file.

MANIAC: (*To phone*) Come on then guess. Who do you think I am... come on play the game... No, no... what do you know? He's guessed it. It is I. Your old mucker Inspector Pietro Anghiari. Well done... What am I doing here in Milan? Ah well... Why don't you tell me what you want with Bertozzo first? ...Well he's indisposed. He's in the rough. Ah the case of the anarchist. Where would that be, sir? ...Political files eh... (*Closes bottom drawer*) ...What exactly have you heard on the grapevine... ?

Opens middle drawer. Rummages.

MANIAC: Ha, ha... The Ministry doesn't trust the motives of the judge who conducted the first enquiry. Rotters, eh. Ha ha... sorry, no you must be very upset, of course... yes, pressure of public opinion... quite a who ha, ha who, who ha, don't mind me sir, just me sense of humour... Yes... ha ha... what a bunch of yellow turds they are in that ministry. First they were delighted and now they are losing their bottle... I see, so this chap is being sent to revise your previous testimony. I find that very interesting, sir. (*Takes*

out file) What's this chap's name? (*Writes*) Professor
Marco Maria Malipiero, and that's the first councillor to
the High Court? You are being honoured. Ha ha ha...
Sorry it's old Bertozzo over there, all this is giving him the
giggles. (*Holds phone away and giggles like Bertozzo.
Phone again*) ...Indeed... (*Away*) Bertozzo, our friend up
there says it's easy for you to laugh but he's in it up to his
neck, have a bit of respect... Yes I've got the files. Your
testimonies, you and er... Superintendent... Verbatim
reports of the torture and interrogations... sorry, slip of the
tongue. Shut up Bertozzo! ...He's having a fit I tell you...
he's creased up... ha ha... No I can't tell you... He says
what's making him laugh is the idea of you two sadists up
there up to your chins in shit... ha ha... Don't get touchy...
(*Blows a huge raspberry down the phone*) That was
Bertozzo blowing you a raspberry. He says you can both
rot for all he cares, you've stood in his way long enough,
about time you were re-posted or pensioned off... Where?
...Where? ...South, probably, some flea-infested station in
the arsehole of the world where the bandits use the fuzz for
target practice when the melons are out of season... ha ha.
OK, I'll tell him. (*Phone away*) ...He says he's going to
push our faces in at the earliest opportunity ha ha... (*To
phone*) You and whose army...? (*Raspberry*) Heil
Himmler!!

*Puts down receiver. Gathers papers. He starts to take off his
disguise. Removing beard and glasses. Rummages in plastic
bag for new stuff.*

MANIAC: To work, at last, a judge. 'Your Honour'. Thank
you. Oh the responsibility. I'm feeling emotional. My day
has come. If I can really convince them that I am the
examining magistrate... must be careful not to make a balls
up of this one. Versatility...! (*Looks in mirror*) ...Yes I see
what you mean.

Tries on a mad disguise. New voice.

MANIAC: 'Ah my dear Inspector, you're not with your old
Nazi pals in the days before the liberation now...' (*To

audience) No? All right, forget it. (*Tries second disguise*) 'What about the vaudeville dancers from the anarchist group in Rome...' (*To Audience*) No...? (*Sees clothing in auditorium. Tries it*) No...? (*Sees coat and hat on coat stand*) Ah! Oh yes. Yes. (*Puts on hat and coat*) Arthritic... but dignified... No, that's no good, that's a registrar... Thirty years for you. (*Starts to walk*) Thirty years for you, forty for you, forty for you etc... fought in the war (*Limps*) ...shell-shock... (*Limps and twitches*) ...what does he do at the weekends? (*Limps, twitches, shoots grouse, twice, third time, limps, shoots and twitches simultaneously*) ...that's how he got his bad eyesight! Ha. (*Tries on monocle*) I'll busk the rest.

Voice off of BERTOZZO .

BERTOZZO: (*Off*) Ah? Constable. I'll just go into my office and use the phone. You bring the files. And while you're at it... etc... etc...

MANIAC *having completed his disguise, replaces beard, enter* BERTOZZO.

BERTOZZO: Hello. Can I... you.

MANIAC: Now don't get neurotic. I just came back for my papers.

BERTOZZO: Out!

MANIAC: Don't take it out on me. I have valuable information. There's this fellow running around says he's going to smash your face in.

BERTOZZO: What?

MANIAC: He hasn't got to you yet? Thank God I've warned you in time. He's fuming. Says he does a nice line in instant plastic surgery.

BERTOZZO: Who?

MANIAC: Your colleague. Who is the one with the fascist boss?

BERTOZZO: Inspector Pissani?

MANIAC: I've struck oil. The very man. He's after you and no mistake.

BERTOZZO: Get out. This is all blather.

He starts to hustle him out.

MANIAC: Take my advice. If you come across him – duck. It's your only hope.

BERTOZZO: OUT!

Exit MANIAC. BERTOZZO *heaves a sigh of relief.*

BERTOZZO: Bloody nutter!

He sees his coat is missing from the coat stand.

BERTOZZO: The shit! He's nicked my coat.

Goes to door. Shouts off.

BERTOZZO: Sergeant!

VOICE OFF: Sir!

BERTOZZO: That man who just left. Get after him!

VOICE OFF: Right away sir!

BERTOZZO *comes back.*

BERTOZZO: What the hell's been going on? (*He looks at his desk*) The charge sheets! Where are they?

Enter CONSTABLE *in the other doorway.*

CONSTABLE: Sir, the Inspector from the political branch is asking for you.

Enter INSPECTOR PISSANI.

BERTOZZO: My dear chap! I was just talking about you, some bloody loony was just telling me that if we ran into each other you were going to... hit me?

INSPECTOR PISSANI *smacks his fist into* BERTOZZO's *face.* BERTOZZO *collapses: Music. Lights.*

Scene Two

Lights up on an office much the same as the first. On the wall a portrait of the President. Window open. The MANIAC, *now disguised as magistrate, puts carrier bag containing a hidden tape recorder under desk and stands by the window. Voices off of* INSPECTOR PISSANI *and* SECOND CONSTABLE. *The* SECOND CONSTABLE *is the same actor only with a moustache.*

CONSTABLE: He stalked in with his nose in the air as if he was the Heavenly Father and says he wants to talk to you and the Superintendent, sir.

PISSANI: I see. Official looking, isn't he?

CONSTABLE: Very.

They enter. PISSANI *is rubbing his hand.*

PISSANI: Good morning. Good morning. What can we do for you?

MANIAC *turns.*

MANIAC: Hurt your hand?

PISSANI: It's nothing.

MANIAC: Why are you rubbing it then? Give yourself a bit of confidence?

PISSANI: To whom do I have the pleasure...

MANIAC *sees* CONSTABLE.

MANIAC: Do I know you?

CONSTABLE: I don't believe so.

MANIAC: (*To* PISSANI) I knew a bishop once, rubbed himself like that. He was a Jesuit of course.

PISSANI: I may be mistaken, but...

MANIAC: You are most certainly mistaken if you assume I am making any kind of allusion to the proverbial hypocrisy of the Jesuits. It may not be relevant at this precise moment but I studied with them, you know. I take it you have no objections.

PISSANI: Er...

MANIAC: Terrific, because you see this bishop to whom I was referring was an inveterate hypocrite. A liar, a cheat and a disgusting lech – always stroking himself, just like you.

PISSANI: Listen!

MANIAC: (*To* CONSTABLE *again*) You got a brother who works here?

CONSTABLE: No.

MANIAC: (*to* STAGE MANAGER) Remind me not to appear in these cheap touring productions again. Can't even afford a decent-sized cast.

VOICE OFF: Sorry (*name of actor*) ...

PISSANI: For Christ's sake. Do you mind?

MANIAC: Sorry, it's the touring.

PISSANI: The greasy breakfasts.

MANIAC: The nylon sheets. Where were we? This continuous massaging, yes, undoubtedly a symptom of insecurity, problems with mater in your formative years I expect. You should screw more. Unleash yourself.

PISSANI: Will you tell me once and for all to whom I have the dubious pleasure of speaking.

MANIAC: I am Professor Marco Maria Malipiero, first councillor to the High Court.

CONSTABLE *gets hand caught in filing cabinet.*

PISSANI: (*Heart attack coming on*) My God, the judge.

CONSTABLE: AAH!

MANIAC: 'Formerly' lecturer at the University of Rome, with two commas and a full stop in the normal way.

PISSANI: We didn't expect you so soon.

MANIAC: Precisely. We decided to catch you on the hop. Does that put you out?

PISSANI: (*struggling to regain his composure*) Not at all.

CONSTABLE: Please sit down, let me take your coat.

MANIAC: You might as well, it's not mine anyway. Please call the Superintendent. I'd like to begin right away.

CONSTABLE *hangs coat and hat on coat stand.*

PISSANI: Perhaps we should go to his office. It's more comfortable.

MANIAC: But isn't this the room where the dirty business with the anarchist took place?

PISSANI: Yes. In here.

MANIAC: (*Spreads his arms and sits*) Well then...

PISSANI: Ask the Superintendent to step in here as quickly as possible if he can...

MANIAC: Even if he can't.

PISSANI: Yes. Even if he can't.

CONSTABLE: Yessir!

Exit CONSTABLE.

PISSANI: I'll just give that bastard Bertozzo a call to bring up the files. No doubt you'll want a transcript of the interrogation.

MANIAC: No, that won't be necessary. I've got everything right here.

PISSANI: Oh.

MANIAC *gets documents out of bags.*

Enter CONSTABLE *and* SUPERINTENDENT.

SUPERINTENDENT: (*Fuming*) Do you know who I've got there?

He's in shirt-sleeves. Sleeves rolled up and carrying a rubber blackjack. Very sweaty.

SUPERINTENDENT: Only bloody Bruno, the Olivetti kidnapper. Only about to crack him, wasn't I, and you send your clodhopping lackey stomping in and screw everything up completely.

PISSANI: I do apologise, but listen…

SUPERINTENDENT: Then I pass poor old Bertozzo on his way to the medical room with a face like some inflatable fruit and learn that you thumped him.

PISSANI: He blew a raspberry at me.

SUPERINTENDENT: Raspberry? Looked more like a prize marrow to me, what did you use? A fucking flagpole? Old Bruno in there looks pristine by comparison.

PISSANI is trying to get a word in.

SUPERINTENDENT: A fine time to start cracking up. Perhaps you don't realise but there are eyes watching us. Press hounds snapping at our heels, waiting for us to slip just once so they can pounce. We must keep our heads.

MANIAC draws SUPERINTENDENT aside.

MANIAC: I share your anxieties, Superintendent.

SUPERINTENDENT: Who the blazes is this?

MANIAC: I have had cause myself to severely reprimand this young associate of yours.. I have noticed he is somewhat repressed, appears to be on the verge of a sexual crisis. Wanking himself stupid I shouldn't wonder. He would benefit greatly from the guidance of an understanding father substitute.

Gives him a visiting card.

MANIAC: Try this man. Fees are a bit steep but he is a genius with arrested adolescents.

SUPERINTENDENT: Who is this dribbling cretin?

PISSANI: Professor Marco Maria Malipiero!

SUPERINTENDENT: What!

PISSANI: First Councillor to the High Court!

SUPERINTENDENT: What!

PISSANI: His honour, the judge is here to conduct the new enquiry...

SUPERINTENDENT: (*To* PISSANI) Why didn't you warn me. (*To* MANIAC) We were expecting you, your Honour, but not so soon.

MANIAC: Caught with your pants down eh?

SUPERINTENDENT: Not at all.

He glares at PISSANI.

PISSANI: I was trying to warn you, Palmi, but you wouldn't let me get a word in.

SUPERINTENDENT: Sir!

PISSANI: Sir.

MANIAC: I should hope so too. Take a tip from your superior, young man. A bit less of the familiar lip, bit more backbone and you wouldn't be coming to pieces at the first hint of hostilities. It's a different school altogether, isn't it Superintendent?

SUPERINTENDENT: You are right, your Honour.

MANIAC: Talking of schools... if you don't mind my saying... your face... it's as if... years ago...

SUPERINTENDENT: What?

MANIAC: Calabria, perhaps.

The SUPERINTENDENT *stiffens with fear.*

SUPERINTENDENT: Calabria?

MANIAC: It is.

He draws the SUPERINTENDENT *downstage. Under his breath.*

MANIAC: 'Forth from the sterilising flame...

SUPERINTENDENT: ...shall burst an instrument of steel.'

MANIAC and SUPERINTENDENT: Ssssh!

> SUPERINTENDENT's *eyes fill with wonder and awe at the* MANIAC. *Comes to attention and clicks his heels. The* MANIAC *winks knowingly. They sing a few bars of the fascist youth song and do a few salutes at each other, giggling.*

MANIAC: Let's keep it to ourselves shall we. Now then, let's get down to the facts.

According to the first transcript of the interrogation... pages 25, 26 and 27... on the evening of, the date's of no importance... 'An anarchist, by profession a railway worker, found himself under interrogation in this very room... on the subject of the bombs planted in railway carriages at the *Milano Centrale Stazione* and more recently the notorious attack at the *Banco Agricoltura* in Milan which caused the deaths of some 17 innocent persons.' Now Superintendent, think carefully. In the report it states you had said: 'There are heavy suspicions pointing in his direction.' Did you say that?

SUPERINTENDENT: Yes, sir. In the beginning... later I said...

MANIAC: Precisely, the beginning. A good enough place to start, don't you agree?

SUPERINTENDENT: Certainly.

MANIAC: Thank you. 'Towards midnight, the anarchist, seized by a "raptus"'... still you speaking... 'seized by a "raptus" threw himself out of the window, thus ending his life upon the pavement below.'

SUPERINTENDENT: Right.

PISSANI: Exactly right.

MANIAC: What is a raptus? Bandieu, in his authoritative work on the subject, states that a 'raptus' is a crisis of suicidal anguish exhibited by a sane person when provoked by a violent anxiety. Right?

BOTH: Right.

MANIAC: Let us see what provoked this anxiety in our anarchist therefore. We shall reconstruct the exact events beginning with your entrance Superintendent.

SUPERINTENDENT: My entrance?

MANIAC: Don't you want to act out your notorious entrance?

SUPERINTENDENT: What notorious entrance?

MANIAC: The entrance that caused the bloody raptus.

SUPERINTENDENT: I didn't make any entrance. It was a junior of mine.

MANIAC: Come, come, it's pretty feeble to pass the buck onto one's inferiors, you know.

PISSANI: You see it was one of these devices that we often employ, in the force, to make the suspect confess.

MANIAC: And who asked your opinion?

PISSANI: No one.

MANIAC: I agree. Speak when you're spoken to, Inspector.

SUPERINTENDENT: It was more or less like this: the suspect, the anarchist was sitting here.

Indicates his own chair. MANIAC *gets* SUPERINTENDENT *up and sits in the chair.*

MANIAC: I'll play the anarchist. Go on.

SUPERINTENDENT: My colleague…

MANIAC: Ah ah.

SUPERINTENDENT: I mean… I… entered.

MANIAC: Go on then.

SUPERINTENDENT: What?

MANIAC: Enter.

SUPERINTENDENT *exits and re-enters. Goes over to* MANIAC.

SUPERINTENDENT: 'It's no use trying to pull the wool over my eyes, sonny.'

MANIAC: That's not what I've got here. This is a documentary reconstruction. I want the exact words in the exact manner.

SUPERINTENDENT *re-exits and re-enters aggressively.*

SUPERINTENDENT: 'Right you filthy pox-ridden pansy you piss me about one more time and I'll... !'

MANIAC: Sorry to interrupt. It was 'piss *me* about'?

SUPERINTENDENT: I think so.

MANIAC: Good. Carry on.

SUPERINTENDENT: 'We've got incontrovertible proof you're the murdering turd who planted the bombs in the railway station.'

MANIAC: You had this proof I assume.

SUPERINTENDENT: Of course not.

MANIAC: Oh dear.

SUPERINTENDENT: That's what the Inspector was trying to explain before, it's just one of those deceptions we're occasionally obliged to resort to...

MANIAC: (*lighting up*) I see! A trap?

PISSANI: Exactly.

MANIAC: Brilliant.

PISSANI: We had our suspicions, however. For a start, the suspect was the only anarchist railway worker in Milan.

SUPERINTENDENT: So it was simple to deduce it was him.

MANIAC: Of course. Of course. It's self-evident. So as it was undoubtedly the case that a *railway worker* must have planted the bomb in the *railway station*, then we can also assert that the famous bombs in the *law courts* must have been planted there by a lawyer, the one at the Agricultural

Bank by a bank clerk or a cow, whichever takes your fancy, and the bomb at the tomb of the Unknown Soldier undoubtedly perpetrated by a corpse.

CONSTABLE: Absolutely.

MANIAC: (*Suddenly furious*) Come along now gentlemen. I'm here to conduct a serious enquiry not fart about with syllogistic prattling. Let's get on with it. It says here: 'Unaffected by the accusations the anarchist smiled disbelievingly.' Who made this statement?

SUPERINTENDENT *and* CONSTABLE *point at* PISSANI. PISSANI *points at* SUPERINTENDENT.

PISSANI: (*Outvoted*) I did, sir.

MANIAC: Good. So there he is smiling disbelievingly. (*Smiles disbelievingly. Looks at notes*) And two lines later I read: 'No doubt fear of getting the sack played a part in precipitating the raptus.' Let's just get this right. First he's smiling disbelievingly, then he's getting the sack so he shits himself and dives out of the window. Well who frightened him?

No answer.

MANIAC: Come on, cops the world over play a few dirty tricks. That's what you're paid for so don't play lily white with me.

BOTH: Thank you, sir.

MANIAC: That's alright. Now who put the frighteners on? Own up. Very well, let me put it another way. You two threaten to tell his boss he's an anarchist, so he will undoubtedly get the sack, this drives the suspect to despair and he leaps out of...

PISSANI: Not so fast.

SUPERINTENDENT: You've misunderstood, your Honour!

PISSANI: I had gone out.

SUPERINTENDENT: But you came back in.

PISSANI: Right.

MANIAC: Drama. Drama. Come on.

CONSTABLE: It was at this point we employed the 'There's-a-phone-call-for-you-sir-it's-very-important' ploy.

Exit CONSTABLE. *Re-enters and addresses* PISSANI.

CONSTABLE: There's a phone call for you sir. It's very important.

PISSANI: Oh. Excuse me, gentlemen.

He exits. Re-enters.

PISSANI: Where? (*Realises he is supposed to be acting*) Oh yes!

Re-exits.

Pause

PISSANI: (*Practising off stage*) 'I've just had a phone call from ROME!' 'I've just HAD a phone call from Rome!' 'I'VE just had a phone call from Rome!'

He re-enters.

PISSANI: (*Very confidently*) I've just had a rome call from Phone. (*His confidence collapses*)

MANIAC: Pregnant pause.

SUPERINTENDENT: He's good isn't he?

MANIAC: Very good. Go on.

PISSANI: '...your friend...'

MANIAC: This is his friend the vaudeville dancer from the anarchist group in Rome.

SUPERINTENDENT: That's right.

MANIAC: The one that strings glass beads together.

PISSANI: That's the one.

MANIAC: (*To audience*) Hilarious, isn't it. Go on.

PISSANI: ' ...your friend, or rather partner, the dancer...'

MANIAC: Did he actually dance in the beads?

PISSANI: What?

MANIAC: The dancer? Probably did. Go on.

PISSANI: ' ...your friend has confessed to planting the bomb in the Milan bank in Rome.'

MANIAC: Christ. How did he take that?

PISSANI: Very badly. He turned pale, asked for a cigarette, lit it, and...

MANIAC: And jumped.

SUPERINTENDENT: Not straightaway.

MANIAC: (*Rounding on the* SUPERINTENDENT) But that's what *you* told the first magistrate.

SUPERINTENDENT: (*Taken aback*) Ah yes.

MANIAC: And then on television you said: 'He loked cornered.' Why was that?

SUPERINTENDENT: Because his alibi had collapsed.

MANIAC: So he didn't jump straightaway?

SUPERINTENDENT: No.

MANIAC: But his alibi had collapsed.

SUPERINTENDENT: Yes.

MANIAC: When?

PISSANI: After he lit his cigarette.

MANIAC: I see.

SUPERINTENDENT: According to his alibi he was supposed to have spent the afternoon of the outrage playing cards in a bar in Naviglia. I said that didn't hold water.

MANIAC: You mean he had no witnesses?

SUPERINTENDENT: He said he did.

MANIAC: But you didn't believe him?

SUPERINTENDENT: Something like that.

MANIAC: Who cares anyway, ha ha. After all, as you told the magistrate: 'The mere *fact* that he jumped was plain admission of guilt.'

SUPERINTENDENT: Absolutely.

MANIAC: And a few weeks later on radio you said: 'Naturally there was no concrete evidence at all against the poor railwayman.' Right?

SUPERINTENDENT: Er...

MANIAC: And on TV, Inspector Pissani you said: 'This anarchist was a good bloke.'

PISSANI: Well things had got a bit out of hand.

MANIAC: I should say.

SUPERINTENDENT: We made a tactical error.

MANIAC: An error? You arrest a free citizen, hold him beyond the legal time limit, and then traumatise him by telling him you have absolute proof that he is a bomber which you later state you didn't have at all, tell him you'll make sure he loses his job, and in spite of three sworn affidavits from witnesses who positively identified this woebegone railwayman as their card-playing colleague in Naviglia you tell him his alibi has collapsed and then you, Inspector, round the whole deal off with the *coup de grâce*; his dearest friend has confessed to a filthy massacre in Rome. Had he?

SUPERINTENDENT: Who?

MANIAC: The dancer.

SUPERINTENDENT: What?

MANIAC: Confessed to planting the bomb in the bank in Rome?

SUPERINTENDENT: No.

MANIAC: No?

PISSANI: We invented it.

MANIAC: What imaginations! Is it any wonder with your incredible inventions battering him from all sides that the suspect is seized with the most enormous raptus and launches himself into space? I'll be frank. You two are done for. You will be charged forthwith with instigating this man to commit suicide.

Both protest.

SUPERINTENDENT: But you admitted yourself our job is to interrogate suspects and we might be required to employ a few intimidating tactics.

MANIAC: We're dealing with a campaign of sustained psychological violence followed by a public exhibition of outrageous and contradictory lies.

PISSANI: But we weren't even in the room when the suicide took place. Ask the Constable!

SUPERINTENDENT *and* PISSANI *drag* CONSTABLE *forward.*

CONSTABLE: Yes, your Honour. They'd both left the room when he threw himself out.

MANIAC: What does that prove? You might as well say an arsonist who primes a bomb and leaves it in a restaurant is innocent because he isn't there when the thing explodes.

PISSANI: Maybe. Yes. With the first version. But the Constable is referring to the second version.

MANIAC: What?

They run and fetch a file.

PISSANI: The second version.

CONSTABLE: What second version do you want?

SUPERINTENDENT: That one.

CONSTABLE: No. That's the second first version.

PISSANI: Well where's the first second version?

CONSTABLE: Here.

All three give file to MANIAC.

ALL THREE: The second version!

MANIAC: So there has been a re-writing of events.

SUPERINTENDENT: A slight correction.

MANIAC: Yes?

SUPERINTENDENT: We corrected the time of the original interrogation in which we employed the...

MANIAC: The lies?

SUPERINTENDENT: ...Er deception strategy. The session ended at eight instead of nearly midnight as previously stated.

MANIAC: You moved everything forward four hours.

PISSANI: Except the fall from the window. There were witnesses to that.

SUPERINTENDENT: We wanted to prove that our 'deceptions' could not have been the determining factor, since four hours had elapsed between the interview and the fall in which the anarchist had fully recovered.

CONSTABLE: (*Taking papers and quoting*) There. 'After an initial period of depression the anarchist was cheering up.'

SUPERINTENDENT: He didn't give a damn about the murdering dancer.

PISSANI: He despised him.

MANIAC: You mean he was in fact aware that the Rome Anarchist group was riddled with police informers and *agents provocateurs* in the pay of neo-fascists.

SUPERINTENDENT: Exactly.

MANIAC: So, since he didn't give a damn about his friend your lies meant nothing to him.

PISSANI: Exactly.

MANIAC: So, why did you tell them to him?

PISSANI: Well it shook him.

MANIAC: It shook him? 'And in no time he was wreathed in smiles.' Your words, Inspector?

PISSANI: He was serene.

MANIAC: So why did he jump? Eh?

They look dumbfounded.

MANIAC: Where's the bleeding raptus gone? Your entire evidence has rested on this raptus. Everyone, including the presiding judge at the original enquiry, has insisted that the poor sod killed himself on account of this uncontrollable raptus and you suddenly give it the elbow.

SUPERINTENDENT: What will we do?

PISSANI: We're doomed.

SUPERINTENDENT: Advise us.

MANIAC: Why do you think I've been sent here? The government has to make some gesture in order to salvage what is left of the mangled reputation of its police force.

PISSANI: What?

MANIAC: The Minister of Internal Affairs and the Minister of Justice have decided that unless you can come up with a miracle you will be made the severest possible example of.

PISSANI: They can't mean to feed us to the wolves.

SUPERINTENDENT: I've sacrificed my life for this country.

MANIAC: They don't give a tinker's fart about your boring bloody sacrifice. This is politics.

PISSANI: We only behaved according to specific directives.

MANIAC: Exactly. 'You must provoke the kind of atmosphere in which we can justifiably demand greater repressive powers.' That's what they told you, right?

PISSANI: They were very persuasive.

SUPERINTENDENT: The subhuman filth are threatening to engulf our beloved country.

MANIAC: 'Society is falling apart.'

SUPERINTENDENT: Action has to be taken. I appeal to your finer instincts, *Kamerad*.

MANIAC: 'Strengthen the state.'

SUPERINTENDENT: Were we wrong?

MANIAC: 'Crack down on hooligans, drop-outs, drunks, addicts, squatters, demonstrators, infiltrate the union militants, round up activists, fatten up the files, polish your rubber bullets... ' But suddenly it's all got out of hand. Somebody has gone too far. Somebody is dead. Outcry and the public wants heads and by God the State had better provide or go under. Your heads, you soppy suckers! You asked for my advice?

SUPERINTENDENT: Yes.

MANIAC *rushes to window and throws it open.*

MANIAC: Out!

PISSANI: What?

MANIAC: The pair of you.

SUPERINTENDENT: No.

MANIAC: Your careers are ruined, your children will spit as you pass, your wives will disown you...

SUPERINTENDENT: It's not fair!

MANIAC: Tradesmen won't serve you! You are abandoned, lost!

PISSANI: This is monstrous! You've had it in for us from the beginning!

MANIAC: Your own ridiculous lies have condemned you!

SUPERINTENDENT: (*To* PISSANI) I warned you, didn't I? 'Leave the script writing to the film directors,' I said; but no, you had to blab your nonsense to the world.

MANIAC: How can you live with the humiliation, Pissani? Your friends, colleagues, your mother laughing in your face.

PISSANI: Ah it's true! Bertozzo has started already!

PISSANI *starts to count rosary beads; he is on his knees.*

MANIAC: Jump, you dishonourable worms!

SUPERINTENDENT: I won't! It's not fair!

MANIAC: Fair? It's the only decent thing left. Follow your victim to oblivion!

PISSANI: He's right!

He climbs onto the window sill.

PISSANI: I can't bear the disgrace! Famiglia, pardona me!

SUPERINTENDENT: No! No! No! There has to be another way!

MANIAC: Can't you feel the raptus boiling up inside you?

PISSANI: Oh oh oooh.

Swaying there, about to jump.

MANIAC: One great liberating leap!

SUPERINTENDENT: (*Suddenly*) I've got it! Don't panic! I've got it!

PISSANI: If I want to panic, I'll panic! I'm going!

As he leaps the SUPERINTENDENT *grabs him and pulls him back in.*

SUPERINTENDENT: A third version!

CONSTABLE: A third version?

MANIAC: What?

SUPERINTENDENT: We'll just have to do a third version!

PISSANI: Haven't we made enough mess of the first two? Let me go!

SUPERINTENDENT: We'll need your help your Honour! The benefit of your keen legal insight and we'll produce a foolproof statement!

PISSANI: Rubbish!

SUPERINTENDENT: Please!

MANIAC: Very well. One last attempt. Get back here, Inspector.

PISSANI: (*Still half hanging out of the window*) I can't.

MANIAC: You'll catch a chill.

CONSTABLE: Are you going or not, sir?

PISSANI: I suppose not.

CONSTABLE helps INSPECTOR in.

MANIAC: Very well. On with the dance: Let's close the shithouse door on all this... (*Shuts the file*) ...as they say, and start all over again.

PISSANI collapses on floor weeping. CONSTABLE puts blanket around his shoulders. Gives him a pill.

SUPERINTENDENT: Point one: what's said cannot be unsaid, therefore it stands that you Inspector and I or someone acting on our behalf played the little deception, the suspect smoked his last fag, but did not throw himself out of the window because it was only eight and not midnight and everyone knows that railwaymen have a great respect for timetables which gives us all the time in the world to change his mood, iron out all the wrinkles and give him a convincing motive for jumping.

MANIAC: I know! You could say that the state of depression into which the anarchist had fallen had moved you.

SUPERINTENDENT: Moved?

MANIAC: Constable!

CONSTABLE: Your Honour?

MANIAC: Were you moved?

CONSTABLE: Moved? I was moved. We were all moved.

MANIAC: You see.

PISSANI: I wasn't moved. I wasn't here.

SUPERINTENDENT: You were.

PISSANI: I was? He was smiling serenely. Why am I moved?

SUPERINTENDENT: He only starts smiling when he sees we are moved?

MANIAC: That's not bad.

SUPERINTENDENT: It's alright.

CONSTABLE: It's good.

MANIAC: It's not good enough.

CONSTABLE: I gave him some chewing gum.

MANIAC: Brilliant. He starts to chew.

SUPERINTENDENT: Then he smiles.

MANIAC: He loves 'Juicyfruit'.

SUPERINTENDENT: And I go out shaking my head.

MANIAC: No! You are still here, too.

SUPERINTENDENT: I am?

PISSANI: (*Testy*) Yes!

MANIAC: Nice try, Superintendent. But you were sorry for having upset him.

SUPERINTENDENT: I felt a certain regret, yes.

MANIAC: And couldn't resist putting a hand on his shoulder.

SUPERINTENDENT: I don't remember that.

MANIAC: A fatherly gesture.

MANIAC *nudges* CONSTABLE.

CONSTABLE: He did, I saw it.

MANIAC: See!

SUPERINTENDENT: Well if he says so...

MANIAC: (*To* PISSANI) And you gave him a gentle pat on the cheek, Inspector.

PISSANI: No... I don't think...

MANIAC: (*Pats his cheek*) Like this.

PISSANI: I'm sorry to disappoint you but...

MANIAC: You are disappointing me. Do you know why?

PISSANI: No.

MANIAC: Because this man was not only an anarchist, but he was also a railwayman. What does that mean to you?

PISSANI: I don't know.

MANIAC: Think. Didn't you have a little train set when you were a nipper?

PISSANI: Yes.

MANIAC: A clockwork one?

PISSANI: Yes. A clockwork armoured train.

MANIAC: How appropriate.

PISSANI: It made real smoke.

MANIAC: Tell me, did it go 'Whoo! Whoo!'

PISSANI: Yes.

MANIAC: Wonderful. How did it go?

PISSANI: Whoo! Whoo!

SUPERINTENDENT: I had one, too.

MANIAC: Let's hear it.

SUPERINTENDENT: Chchch Whoo – ch chWhoo Whoo!

MANIAC: (*Singing*) Pardon me boys –

ALL: Is that the Chatenuga choo choo. Whoo! Whoo!

MANIAC: Wonderful! Wonderful! I bet your eyes sparkled! How could you have felt anything but affection for this man, this railwayman, bound forever in your subconscious mind to the little train sets of your childhood. I'm more than certain you gave his cheek a little pat. (*Nudging* CONSTABLE *again*)

CONSTABLE: It's true. I saw him. He did.

MANIAC: You see. And you said: 'There, there, my lad, don't take it like that!' And you called him by his Christian name.

PISSANI: I certainly did not…

MANIAC: Don't make me lose my temper.

PISSANI: Very well.

SUPERINTENDENT: Let's get it down, word for word.

CONSTABLE *sits to write.*

SUPERINTENDENT: He said: 'Come along now, my lad...'

CONSTABLE: (*As he writes*) 'Come along now, my lad.'

SUPERINTENDENT: ' ...Don't take it like that.'

CONSTABLE: 'Don't take it like that.'

MANIAC: And then we began to sing.

CONSTABLE: 'And then we began to... ' Sing?

PISSANI: What?

MANIAC: You began to sing. All of you.

SUPERINTENDENT: Sing?

MANIAC: Of course. Doesn't it make sense? Having created such a cosy atmosphere what else would you do but engage yourselves in four-part harmony?

SUPERINTENDENT: Your Honour, we can't possibly go along with this.

MANIAC: Then don't. I wash my hands of you! There's the window. It's the only viable alternative. First you cook up one story, then you cook up another, and neither of you can agree on either one and both are masterpieces of incompetence. Who believes anything you say? No one. Why? Because besides being evident garbage your stories lack the tiniest vestige of humanity. No warmth. No laughter. No pain. No remorse. SING! (*Guitars*) For God's sake. Show a human heart beating beyond the sordid tangle of lies you have left in your wake. Before it is too late, give the public something to believe in. SING! (*Cast begin to sing*) Sing and they may forgive the superficial facts. Three tortured human souls, albeit they are policemen, singing their suspect's song with him to cheer him through his darkest hour. The song of anarchy itself. 'Our homeland is the whole world. Our law is liberty. We have but one thought, revolution in our hearts.'

Raminghi per le terre
E per i mari
Per un'idea lasciamo
I nostri cari

CHORUS:

Nostra patria è il mondo intero
Nostra legge è la libertà
Ed un pensiero, ed un pensiero
Nostra patria è il mondo intero
Nostra legge è la libertà
Ed un pensiero
Ribelle in cuor ci sta

Ma torneranno, Italia
I tuoi coscritti
Ad agitar la pace
Dei diritti

CHORUS:

Nostra patria... etc.

MANIAC *announces interval in Italian.*

Act Two
Scene One

Scene: the same.

The four take up their singing where they left off at the end of Act One, finishing as the lights come up to full.

They applaud each other, hug, kiss hands etc.

ALL: Bravo! Well done! Magnificent!

Knock on door right. STAGE MANAGER *with tray and coffee, handed to* CONSTABLE.

MANIAC: Excellent! So here we are, and our suspect is in the best of moods.

PISSANI: He's never been happier.

SUPERINTENDENT: He's ecstatic.

CONSTABLE: Coffee, gentlemen.

ALL: Ah coffee.

CONSTABLE: The suspect was serene.

SUPERINTENDENT: Ha, ha, yes serene.

ALL: (*Singing*) He was serene.

PISSANI: Exactly.

SUPERINTENDENT: The crossfire of false accusations hasn't in the least upset his mental state.

MANIAC: No raptus?

SUPERINTENDENT: Not a whisper of stress.

PISSANI: All that is much later.

CONSTABLE: At midnight.

MANIAC: Fine. And now it's midnight.

THREE POLICEMEN: (*Suddenly deflated*) Oh!

MANIAC: Constable?

CONSTABLE: Your Honour?

MANIAC: Set the scene.

CONSTABLE: (*Hesitant*) Er... it's midnight...

MANIAC *makes an owl noise. Others help create midnight atmosphere.*

CONSTABLE: ...there are five of us in this room... the suspect, myself, and another constable and...

SUPERINTENDENT: ...I'd just stepped out...

MANIAC: Sssh!

CONSTABLE: And... er...

MANIAC: Those two?

CONSTABLE: Yes.

PISSANI *glares at* CONSTABLE.

MANIAC: What are they doing?

CONSTABLE: Interrogating the suspect.

MANIAC: Still? After all these hours? Must be knackered! 'Where were you on the night of... ?' 'Don't play dumb with me' and on and on, dear God but you must be exasperated.

PISSANI: Just a bit.

MANIAC: I expect you fancy roughing him up a bit?

PISSANI: Never touched the bastard.

SUPERINTENDENT: Very even tempered. The whole proceedings.

MANIAC: Don't get me wrong. Just a little slap, pchew!, across the chops?

PISSANI: Never got near him.

MANIAC: Bit of a massage, to relieve his tensions...

MANIAC starts to massage CONSTABLE.

MANIAC: ...shoulders full of cramps... yes...

CONSTABLE: Left a bit.

MANIAC: Left a bit. There.

CONSTABLE: Lovely.

MANIAC: ...After all those hours... and then...

Sudden karate chop.

MANIAC: ...Ka...

Karate act.

MANIAC: ...Ka! Ya! Eeeeaaah!

PISSANI: (*Very indignant*) There was no violence, no massage, no karate, nothing like that. It was all above board according to regulations. We were conducting our enquiries in a very lighthearted manner.

MANIAC: You *were* interrogating him?

PISSANI: Lightheartedly.

SUPERINTENDENT: We were having a bit of a laugh with him.

MANIAC: Playing 'Grandmother's footsteps' were you? Paper hats? Stick the tail on the donkey?

CONSTABLE: It was just the odd joke, your Honour, you should see the Inspector when he's on form. Keeps us all in stitches. Ha ha.

MANIAC: Especially when interrogating mass-murder suspects.

CONSTABLE: Especially then. Ha. Er...

MANIAC: So you're a bit of a wag, Inspector.

PISSANI: Well...

MANIAC: Don't be modest. Take the stage. Give us a quick dose.

CONSTABLE: Go on sir.

PISSANI *tells jokes. Takes applause.*

MANIAC: Did you tell the suspect that one?

PISSANI: Yes.

MANIAC: No wonder he jumped. No seriously, Inspector, seriously. You see all this jocular banter explains a great deal that has often worried me. For instance, I was holidaying in Bergamo a couple of summers back during the time of the notorious 'Monday Gang' affair, if you recall? Practically everyone in the village was under arrest, the café proprietor, the doctor, even the priest; (*in nomine, spiritu sancti*, you're nicked); of course in the end they all turned out to be innocent. Still, my hotel, you see, was right next to the police station and I simply could not get a wink of sleep the whole time I was there for the shrieks and screams and slappings and loud thuds. Naturally, I assumed as any citizen who reads the papers and watches TV would, that these were the sounds of suspects being beaten under interrogation by brutal country coppers. All too clearly now I can see how mistaken my impressions were. Those shrieks I heard were shrieks of laughter, the screams were screams of merriment and mirth accompanied by thigh slapping convulsions of humorous hysteria:

Thrashes about laughing and miming being beaten.

MANIAC: 'Hahahaha! Jeeesus! No! That's enough! I've heard that one before. Help! Haha, no more! I love a party. Don't you?' I can see it all. The wackey, witty *carabinieri*. Those southerners…

Mimes broken nose and cauliflower ear.

MANIAC: …what jokers …sending their suspects spinning across the floor in fits of fun, smashing their heads on the tiles at the side-splitting japes:

Does somersault as result of imaginary blow in stomach.

MANIAC: 'Ha, stop it! Ha ha! No! Please! Mercy! I can't take any more!'

The THREE POLICEMEN *have joined in the act,*

shouting and miming various tortures. MANIAC *suddenly turns on them.*

MANIAC: This explains why so many perfectly ordinary, bored people suddenly dress themselves up as anarchists and revolutionaries – they are completely innocent, they just want to get themselves arrested so they can have a fucking good laugh for once in their lives. Our cunning anarchist is obviously in his grave right now, pissing himself!

Pause. The irony has got through.

PISSANI: I don't understand. You said you were going to help us and all you do is pour scorn and derision on our heads. We sang. We showed you how warm and human we are.

MANIAC: I promise not to make fun of you any more. Absolute seriousness from now on. Let us get down to the true and proper point, the suspect's leap.

PISSANI: Right.

MANIAC: Even though we can't seem to find a credible motive for the idiotic act at the moment. Never mind. Our anarchist, seized by a psychological crisis of some kind suddenly jumps up, takes a short run and... just a sec... who gave him a leg up?

SUPERINTENDENT: What do you mean?

MANIAC: You know...

Goes to window and demonstrates with fingers interlocked.

MANIAC: ...over the sill and into the void... bit of a jump that, isn't it? You'd need a good run at that.

SUPERINTENDENT: Your Honour is surely not suggesting that...

MANIAC: Springboard handy, was there? A little baby trampoline, something of that ilk?

SUPERINTENDENT: You're at it again!

MANIAC: Just sifting the evidence. Maybe he had springs in his heels like Beau Brummel.

PISSANI: He had no ruddy springs in his bloody heels!

MANIAC: Fine. All right. *But* here was a man of 5 foot 4, give or take an inch, on his own, without stepladder, spring, accomplice, trampoline, bri-nylon rope with crampons attached or any other device and he manages to get from there... (*Indicates chair, indicates window*) ...to here and within three seconds he becomes jam sponge and there's four highly-trained policemen just standing there. Look at the room, gentlemen. Surely one of you must have been in the vicinity of the window.

PISSANI: It all happened very quickly.

CONSTABLE: He was very athletic. Very fast.

MANIAC: I see.

CONSTABLE: I only just managed to grab him by the foot.

MANIAC: Ah ha! My tenacity pays off, you see. You grabbed him by the foot?

CONSTABLE: Yes, but his shoe just came off in my hand.

MANIAC: That's it! Brilliant! Why didn't I see it before? The vital thing was you had the shoe in your hand. Incontrovertible proof of your efforts to save the suspect. You've done it, gentlemen. Well done, Constable.

They slowly twig they are in the clear.

PISSANI: Of course! It works.

SUPERINTENDENT: Well done, Constable!

PISSANI *and* SUPERINTENDENT *take drinks from filing cabinet, applaud and shake the* CONSTABLE's *hand.*

CONSTABLE: Thank you, Super, thank you, sir.

MANIAC: Just a minute. Sorry.

Everyone freezes.

MANIAC: There's one little detail doesn't quite fit here

(*Looking at papers*) Was the suspect a triped, Superintendent?

SUPERINTENDENT: (*Relief turning to boiling rage*) I beg your pardon?

MANIAC: This suicidal railwayman. If by chance the bugger's got three fee‹, we're home and dry.

SUPERINTENDENT *nearly explodes.*

MANIAC: Temper! Temper! It'll end in tears. You see according to page 5 of the judge's evidence the Constable states, as he has just done, that he had the anarchist's shoe in his hand... But according to this addendum on page 16, four witnesses in the courtyard below, including a reporter from *Corriere della Sera*, swear the jam sponge was accoutred with a pair of shoes consistent with the average biped.

SUPERINTENDENT: Well that's a funny business.

MANIAC: To be sure.

PISSANI: Don't know how that's happened.

MANIAC: Unless the Constable here, moving like the clappers, had time to belt down to the balcony a few floors below, lean out and slip the suspect's shoe back on as he came sailing by.

PISSANI: Jesus!!

MANIAC: Well you find a plausible explanation!

PISSANI: (*Beside himself with panic*) Very well. Obviously one of the suspect's shoes must have been too big for him – so, not having an insole to hand, he had previously put a smaller shoe on inside the bigger one which came off in the Constable's hand! Or one foot was considerably smaller than the other and the same means was employed to even-up the feet for cosmetic reasons!

Pause. PISSANI *looks manically triumphant.* MANIAC *sits back to enjoy the scene.*

SUPERINTENDENT: Two shoes on one foot?

PISSANI: Precisely.

CONSTABLE: It's not as mad as it sounds, sir.

SUPERINTENDENT: It's fucking deranged! There's no mention in the autopsy of abnormally disproportioned feet.

CONSTABLE: That's not the point I'm pursuing. I'm saying that what I held in my hand may, in fact, have been a galosh.

SUPERINTENDENT: Nobody wears galoshes these days.

PISSANI: Anyway, it wasn't raining.

CONSTABLE: Ah, but the anarchist may have thought it was about to.

SUPERINTENDENT: Galoshes are a ridiculous garment. An anarchist wouldn't be seen dead in them.

CONSTABLE: Exactly!

SUPERINTENDENT: Bloody balls, Constable.

CONSTABLE: Only trying to help.

SUPERINTENDENT: Cock! Complete cock!

PISSANI: Anarchists are often very eccentric; he may well have been wearing galoshes.

SUPERINTENDENT: Well where are they? Where are the fucking galoshes? Not in the transcript, not amongst the dead man's possessions, the shoe he had in his hand was a shoe...

Runs to get a cardboard box. Empties dead man's possessions on floor.

SUPERINTENDENT: ...this shoe, which you... (*Waves shoe at* PISSANI) ... secretly put there after we'd first given evidence.

PISSANI:
CONSTABLE: } Ssssssshhhhh!!!

SUPERINTENDENT: I will not shush! Look, look, look there's its little tag... item 99b: one shoe. Not galosh! Pinheads! Whose writing is that?

PISSANI: I only did it on your orders!

SUPERINTENDENT: Me!? Me?! You weren't involved all of a sudden.

CONSTABLE: Please! Sir!

SUPERINTENDENT: Keep out of it! It's all me now! You didn't enjoy yourself, of course?!

PISSANI: I was having a laugh. Yes. You said that, didn't you Constable!

CONSTABLE: Yes.

SUPERINTENDENT: Some laugh! Ha! Laughing now, aren't we?!

PISSANI: I was just scaring him. *You* are the nutter!

SUPERINTENDENT: I'm a nutter!?

CONSTABLE: Please.

PISSANI: Well you bloody pushed him, chum!

SUPERINTENDENT: Did I? Did I? That is a laugh alright! All on my own, was I!

Suddenly all three realise at the same instant that the MANIAC *is listening. They freeze. Slowly turn. The* MANIAC *has a beatific smile. Pause. No one speaks.*

Phone shatters the silence. It rings. No one moves.

MANIAC: Better answer it.

PISSANI: But you...

MANIAC: I never heard a word, Inspector.

PISSANI *picks up receiver.*

PISSANI: (*On phone*) Hello... Just a minute... (*To* SUPERINTENDENT) Some journalist for you. She's waiting downstairs.

SUPERINTENDENT: My God, it's that Feletti woman from *L'Unità*. I'd forgotten I told her we'd see her today.

PISSANI: Not about this business, surely?

SUPERINTENDENT: What else? I didn't have any choice. City Hall ordered me to see her and try to quieten her down.

PISSANI: I've read her stuff. She's a bloody viper.

MANIAC: Well you'd better see her then. Don't want to get her back up any more.

SUPERINTENDENT: What about your enquiry?

MANIAC: It'll have to wait.

SUPERINTENDENT: If you wait in my office we'll get rid of her as quickly as possible.

MANIAC: I'm fine right here.

PISSANI: But if she finds out who you are it could ruin everything.

SUPERINTENDENT: On the other hand the Professor's quick thinking would be an invaluable asset if she starts slinging loaded questions.

PISSANI: The main thing is that we aren't compromised.

SUPERINTENDENT: Constable clear this mess up.

CONSTABLE: Right away, Superintendent.

MANIAC: I'll just stay in the background. You tip me the wink if you want me to stick my oar in.

SUPERINTENDENT: You are too kind, your Honour.

PISSANI: You see, one 'your Honour' and we're done for.

CONSTABLE: Can't the Professor pretend to be someone else?

PISSANI: What?

SUPERINTENDENT: Wonderful idea!

MANIAC: Yes! I could be a psychiatrist from the criminal department.

CONSTABLE: Terrific.

SUPERINTENDENT: No no no. I know. Captain

Marcantonio Banzi Piccini. He's a friend of mine in forensics from Rome.

CONSTABLE: Even better.

CONSTABLE *exits*.

SUPERINTENDENT: If she says anything defamatory in her article afterwards we can call him in as a witness. Ha.

PISSANI: Can you bluff your way in forensics?

MANIAC: No problem. I'll need a disguise of course. Can't work without costume.

SUPERINTENDENT: Oh dear.

MANIAC: Not to worry. I have some stuff right here.

SUPERINTENDENT: *Cristo Dio*.

MANIAC *goes out door left*. CONSTABLE *re-enters*.

SUPERINTENDENT: (*To* PISSANI) Better send her up. (*To* CONSTABLE) Constable meet her at the top of the stairs.

Exit CONSTABLE.

PISSANI: (*To phone*) OK. Send her up.

PISSANI *puts down receiver. Re-enter* MANIAC *with carrier bags*.

MANIAC: I'll just change in there.

SUPERINTENDENT: You don't know how much we appreciate this, your Honour.

MANIAC: Never let it be said I would abandon my friends in their hour of need.

Goes out of door, stage left.

SUPERINTENDENT: That man is a genius.

PISSANI: I'm not at all sure about this.

Knock at door stage right.

PISSANI: Come!

Re-enter CONSTABLE *with* MARIA FELETTI.

CONSTABLE: Maria Feletti, sir.

PISSANI: Miss Feletti, delighted...

SUPERINTENDENT: ...to meet you. I'm the Superintendent. We spoke on the telephone. Allow me to introduce my colleague Inspector Pissani in charge of this department.

FELETTI: Pleased to meet you.

PISSANI: The pleasure is all mine.

He shakes her hand.

SUPERINTENDENT: Do sit down.

FELETTI: Thank you. I shan't beat about the bush. As you may be aware, my paper has been less than enthusiastic about the flagrant public white-washing given to recent events in this building by the City Magistrate's offic.

SUPERINTENDENT: This may be because your paper prefers to deal in rumour rather than fact. If I may say so without being personal, Miss Feletti.

FELETTI: I doubt it.

SUPERINTENDENT: Even so I have read your column with admiration. You have struck me as a woman of great courage, a true democrat and lover of justice.

FELETTI: You are too kind. I wonder if I could begin by asking the Inspector a couple of questions.

PISSANI: Certainly.

FELETTI: Why do people call you the 'Window Straddler'?

PISSANI: I beg your pardon?

FELETTI: (*Taking out a paper*) This is a copy of a letter written by a young anarchist now in San Vittore prison... 'The Inspector on the fourth floor forced me to sit on the window sill with my legs hanging out. "Throw yourself out!" he said and "Jump! Go on. Or haven't you got the guts!" He threatened to push me. I was terrified.'

PISSANI: I resent this.

SUPERINTENDENT: (*Calm and indifferent*) Marco will be

here in a minute.

PISSANI: Oh, it's Marco now is it?

FELETTI: You were saying?

SUPERINTENDENT: If you attach any importance to the words of a condemned man against those of a police officer I'm afraid I don't know how to respond.

MANIAC: (*Off*) Superintendent!

SUPERINTENDENT: Ah, perhaps my colleague can help. I took the liberty of inviting him to join us. A forensic expert from Rome. Come in!

Captain Marcantonio Banzi Piccini, may I present Maria Feletti from the...

He dries up as he turns to come face to face with the MANIAC. MARIA FELETTI *and* PISSANI *have risen to their feet and stare open-mouthed, as does the* CONSTABLE. *The* MANIAC *is outrageously costumed. He wears false moustache, glasses, wild wig, wooden leg, false hand, eye patch, carries a crutch.*

MANIAC: Delighted!

He proffers his false hand.

MANIAC: Pardon my stiff hand. It's wooden. Memento of the Algerian campaign. Nasty business. We don't talk about it.

They stare at his wooden leg. He gives it a slap.

MANIAC: Vietnam. Green Berets. All past history. Do sit down.

Slowly they all sit.

MANIAC: (*To Audience*) No cigarettes please. All dry wood here. Right, young woman, don't mind me. I'll just park my old timbers over here and you get stuck in. What's the subject?

FELETTI: Window straddling.

MANIAC: (*He sits awkwardly*) Splendid.

FELETTI: According to the evidence of the emergency services a call was registered from the switchboard of this station on the night of the alleged suicide at two minutes *to* twelve. The call was a request for ambulance services. Witnesses to the suicide all agreed it took place at three minutes *past* twelve. Can you explain this discrepancy?

SUPERINTENDENT: It is a crime to be prudent and show a bit of foresight, now, is it?

PISSANI: We sometimes call an ambulance on the off-chance.

SUPERINTENDENT: Anyway the clock that registered our call in the exchange was probably slow.

PISSANI: More than likely.

FELETTI: Extraordinary.

MANIAC: Why extraordinary? This is not Switzerland, you know. People set their clocks as they bloody well like here. Some forward, some back. We live in a country of artists and stupendous individualists. We are Italians. Rebels against habit and custom.

SUPERINTENDENT: Well said, Captain.

He slaps MANIAC *on back.*

MANIAC: Mind the eye.

SUPERINTENDENT: Eye?

MANIAC: It's glass. You'll knock it out.

SUPERINTENDENT: Oh sorry.

PISSANI: What are you driving at Miss Feletti?

FELETTI: Among the documents of the enquiry produced by the investigating judge, there is no sign of any expert analysis of the parabola of the fall. Something almost obligatory in such cases.

SUPERINTENDENT: Parabola?

PISSANI: Parabola?

MANIAC: Beautiful word.

FELETTI: It would establish whether or not the anarchist was still alive when he went through the window; i.e. did he go through it with a slight jerk indicating a voluntary movement which would clear the side of the building, or did he, as appears, slide down the wall sustaining fractures and lesions consistent with an inanimate object? Were the suicide's hands injured in such a way as to indicate he put them out to protect himself instinctively at the moment of impact? This would indicate whether he was conscious or not.

MANIAC: I think I ought to point out that we're dealing with a case of suicide. The bastard wanted to die so why the hell would he put his bloody hands out?

SUPERINTENDENT: Splendidly answered.

Slaps MANIAC's back.

MANIAC: The eye. Mind the eye, can't you?

FELETTI: Perhaps you can explain the bruises seen on the young man's neck. It's not at all clear what caused those.

SUPERINTENDENT: I advise you against careless talk, young lady.

FELETTI: Is that a threat?

MANIAC: Not at all. Not at all, no. You see there were indeed bruises on the anarchist's neck. These were caused during the final interrogation just before midnight. One of the policemen became slightly impatient and struck the suspect a hard blow on the nape of the neck.

FELETTI: Ah!

SUPERINTENDENT: What?!

MANIAC: Regrettable, but true.

PISSANI: Have you gone mad?

MANIAC: Sixteen times precisely. The suspect was partially paralysed by the blow and had momentary difficulty breathing. An ambulance was called immediately. At the same time two officers assisted the anarchist to the open window, supporting him as he leant out to take in a few reviving gulps of cold night air. Now, as is often the case in such events, each of the officers thought the other had the stronger hold, you know the sort of thing – 'To me Giacomo' – 'OK Batista!' and whoops, out he goes! What more can you say?

The simple explanation floors FELETTI *who slumps back in her chair.*

SUPERINTENDENT: Brilliant!

PISSANI: Superb!

SUPERINTENDENT: So simple!

PISSANI: Classic!

SUPERINTENDENT: Well done, Captain!

Slaps his back. A loud plop.

MANIAC: That's it!

SUPERINTENDENT: Fuck me!

MANIAC: What did I tell you? It's gone.

PISSANI: What?

SUPERINTENDENT: Oh good heavens!

MANIAC: The eye's out! Everybody down!

CONSTABLE, SUPERINTENDENT *and* PISSANI *crawl around looking for the eye.*

FELETTI: A very clever explanation, Captain.

MANIAC: Not bad. But the brain-work gives you a headache, what!

FELETTI: I have to admit that this version clarifies several points.

MANIAC: Why the ambulance was called in advance; the inanimate fall of the body...

FELETTI: ...and the strange terminology employed by the judge in his summing up.

SUPERINTENDENT: What strange terminology?

MANIAC: Yes, try to be more precise, madam. (*To* PISSANI) Have you found it yet?

PISSANI: What colour is it?

SUPERINTENDENT: It's see-through, you dumbo. It's an eye.

FELETTI: What I am saying is the verdict of the enquiry was that the anarchist's death was 'accidental' as opposed to the police claim of 'suicide'.

Knock at the door stage right. CONSTABLE *is crawling by the door.* PISSANI *on the other side of the desk.*

PISSANI: Come in!

Door bursts open, sending CONSTABLE *flying. It is* BERTOZZO. *He holds a metallic package. Also wears an eye patch.*

SUPERINTENDENT: Ah Bertozzo!

BERTOZZO: Oh, sorry. Am I interrupting? I just came to deliver this.

SUPERINTENDENT: What is it?

CONSTABLE: My nose!

BERTOZZO: It's a reproduction of the bomb that went off in the Agricultural Bank.

SUPERINTENDENT: Splendid. Stick it on the desk, there, would you.

PISSANI: Found it!

MANIAC: Where?

It is too late to retrieve the eye before it is stepped on by BERTOZZO, *on his way to the desk. It sends him flying. As his legs go from under him the bomb flies up in the air.*

SUPERINTENDENT: The bomb!!

FELETTI *screams.* CONSTABLE *hits the deck.* MANIAC *catches the bomb.* PISSANI *grabs the eye.*

MANIAC: Owzat!

PISSANI: Got you!

Everyone rigid with horror except MANIAC *and* PISSANI.

BERTOZZO: What the hell was that?

MANIAC: My eye. This yours?

He tosses bomb to BERTOZZO. *Everyone screams.*
BERTOZZO *catches bomb.*

BERTOZZO: Don't be alarmed. There's no detonator.

FELETTI: Thank God for that.

PISSANI *gives* MANIAC *his eye.*

MANIAC: Look what a mess you've made of it. Constable would you be kind enough to get me a glass of water to wash it in?

CONSTABLE: Certainly.

Exit CONSTABLE.

BERTOZZO: (*To* MANIAC) Your face looks very familiar.

MANIAC: That'll be because we've both got bandaged eyes.

SUPERINTENDENT: Please allow me to introduce you. Inspector Bertozzo, Captain Marcantonio Piccini of the forensic department.

BERTOZZO: Piccini? That's impossible. I know Captain Piccini.

PISSANI *kicks* BERTOZZO.

PISSANI: Oh no you don't!

BERTOZZO *sees* PISSANI *for the first time.*

BERTOZZO: You! You kicked me. You're assaulting me again. Why?

SUPERINTENDENT: That's quite enough.

BERTOZZO: I want to know why you punched me in the eye.

SUPERINTENDENT: He didn't punch you. He kicked you.

PISSANI: Because of the insults and the raspberry.

BERTOZZO: What raspberry?

SUPERINTENDENT: That's enough!!

MANIAC: My mind's reeling.

SUPERINTENDENT: (*Indicates* FELETTI) Can't you see we have visitors?

BERTOZZO: (*Meaning* MANIAC) Very well and that is not Captain...

SUPERINTENDENT *kicks* BERTOZZO.

SUPERINTENDENT: ...Piccini!

PISSANI: Got it?

BERTOZZO: No.

SUPERINTENDENT *kicks* BERTOZZO.

SUPERINTENDENT: Piccini!

BERTOZZO *screams in frustration. Enter* CONSTABLE *with glass of water.*

CONSTABLE: Your glass of water, sir.

MANIAC: Thank you.

SUPERINTENDENT: And this is Miss Feletti.

PISSANI: (*In* BERTOZZO's *ear*) We'll explain later.

SUPERINTENDENT: (*Very pointed*) Miss Feletti is a journalist.

PISSANI: (*Still in his ear*) Understand now?

BERTOZZO: No.

SUPERINTENDENT: She's here for an important interview.

SUPERINTENDENT *winks.* MANIAC *drops eye in glass of water and shakes it.*

PISSANI: See.

FELETTI: How do you do?

BERTOZZO *is gaga. They shake hands.* MANIAC *swallows his eye like a pill.*

MANIAC: Aah!

CONSTABLE: What now?

MANIAC: I've swallowed my eye.

SUPERINTENDENT: Inspector Bertozzo is our explosives and ballistics expert.

FELETTI: Oh really.

MANIAC: Well I hope it cures the headache.

FELETTI: I wonder if I could ask the Inspector some questions?

BERTOZZO: Of course.

FELETTI: I am struck by a curious thing. You say this is a reproduction of the bomb used at the Agricultural Bank.

BERTOZZO: Based on fragments found in the wreckage, yes.

FELETTI: So although it's a real bomb it doesn't carry the same information concerning its maker as the original would have done?

BERTOZZO: The original may have been constructed differently.

FELETTI: I believe the saying goes: 'Tell me how you make a bomb and I'll tell you *who* you are.'

BERTOZZO: There's some truth in that.

FELETTI: The unmistakable signature of the bombers is lost with the explosion?

BERTOZZO: Nine times out of ten, yes.

FELETTI: Wasn't one of the recent wave of bombs recovered unexploded?

SUPERINTENDENT: Mmmmmmm!

BERTOZZO: The one at the Commercial Bank. Yes.

SUPERINTENDENT: Mmmmmmnnn!

PISSANI: (*Under his breath to* BERTOZZO) Easy.

FELETTI: Can you explain why within minutes of the discovery of this potential harvest of hard evidence an officer from this building exploded the device when the normal procedure, I understand, is to dismantle such things in a laboratory?

PISSANI *and* SUPERINTENDENT *look nervous.*

PISSANI:
SUPERINTENDENT: } 'Tsssssss!'

BERTOZZO: Well I... I'm not sure if I understand...

SUPERINTENDENT: Mnnnn!

MANIAC *steps forward and picks up the bomb.*

MANIAC: Perhaps you'll allow me a word here, Inspector Bertozzo, in my capacity as chief of the forensic department.

BERTOZZO: What's he doing? Put that down. It's dangerous.

MANIAC: No, no. It's quite safe, Miss Feletti.

BERTOZZO: I'm telling you he is not... (PISSANI *and* SUPERINTENDENT *stamp on his feet*) Aah!

PISSANI: We know.

BERTOZZO: Well who is he... (*Again*) ...aah!

MANIAC *has started to unscrew top of bomb.*

CONSTABLE: You do know what you're doing, don't you, your Honour?

MANIAC: (*To* CONSTABLE) Haven't got the foggiest idea. (*To* FELETTI) You see here, Miss Feletti, a bomb like this is complex, tons of wire in there, always a good sign. Ah, now this here is a priming device, could even be a double-timing priming device, some form of acid booby trap, we just don't know, you see...

SUPERINTENDENT: (*To* BERTOZZO) Sounds like an expert, eh?

MANIAC: ...could take a day dismantling the first phase meanwhile BOOM!

He tosses bomb in air. All scream and dive for cover. He catches it.

MANIAC: Better to lose the evidence than risk the added carnage, don't you agree?

FELETTI: I'm convinced.

SUPERINTENDENT: So am I.

MANIAC: I've even convinced myself. Not bad, eh?

SUPERINTENDENT: Well done! Brilliant!

Starts to shake MANIAC's *hand. It comes off.*

MANIAC: I told you it was only wood.

Snatches it back and screws it on again.

PISSANI: Say something, Bertozzo.

SUPERINTENDENT: Show we're not asleep in this section.

BERTOZZO: Er... the original bomb was highly complex.

FELETTI: Even more complex than this?

BERTOZZO: Oh absolutely, certainly. Obviously the work of a professional.

PISSANI *and* SUPERINTENDENT *shake their heads at* BERTOZZO.

FELETTI: A military man perhaps?

BERTOZZO: More than likely.

PISSANI *and* SUPERINTENDENT *kick him mercilessly.*

BERTOZZO: What have I done now?!!!

FELETTI: So! Notwithstanding knowing that to handle, let alone make, bombs of this kind probably requires military skill, you completely ignored all other avenues of investigation and concentrated your entire effort on the most pathetic and disorganised group of anarchists in Italy.

SUPERINTENDENT: Pathetic they may look, but their disorganisation is only a cunning façade.

FELETTI: And what do we find behind this cunning façade, Superintendent? I'll tell you. A group of ten, one of whom was a spy employed by this office, two detectives from the crime squad, and a fourth member turns out to be a notorious fascist well known to everyone except this feeble bunch of anarchists. How many more government employees have you got scattered amongst the far left?

SUPERINTENDENT: I make no bones about the use of paid informers. They are the secret of our strength.

PISSANI: Our eyes and ears, they warn us, keep things under control.

FELETTI: Indeed? If you were in such complete control of this little bunch, Inspector, how were they able to conduct such a sophisticated operation without your even knowing of it, let alone intervening to prevent it?

PISSANI: At the time the incident was being planned our officer was absent from the group.

SUPERINTENDENT: True.

MANIAC: He had a note from his mother.

BERTOZZO: (*To audience*) He's too clever by half.

FELETTI: What about the other informer? The fascist.

BERTOZZO: (*To audience*) I'm sure I've seen him before.

SUPERINTENDENT: He was most certainly *not* one of our informers.

FELETTI: (*Takes out photographs and confronts* SUPERINTENDENT) So why are the press publishing photographs of him coming and going at police headquarters in Rome?

MANIAC: Well done, Miss Feletti. Admit it Superintendent, she's drawn blood.

MANIAC *shakes* FELETTI's *hand*.

FELETTI: Thank you.

BERTOZZO: (*To audience*) He's getting up my nose.

MANIAC's *hand comes off in* FELETTI's.

FELETTI: Oh, your hand.

MANIAC: Keep it. I've got a spare.

Rummages in his carrier bag.

BERTOZZO: I know him. I tell you I know him.

SUPERINTENDENT: So do we.

BERTOZZO: Then why are you allowing this... aaaAAAHHH!

PISSANI and SUPERINTENDENT *stand on a foot each.* MANIAC *produces another hand. Elegant, manicured, with nails varnished.*

FELETTI: It's a woman's.

MANIAC: It's unisex.

He screws it on. FELETTI *throws hand over her shoulder in revulsion. It lands in filing cabinet as* CONSTABLE *is closing drawer. His fingers get mashed.*

CONSTABLE: AAAH!

SUPERINTENDENT: This woman is getting out of hand.

PISSANI: Your Honour... !

FELETTI: (*Desperately clinging to her performance*) Listen!! There have been 173 dynamite attacks in the last fourteen months, that's twelve a month, one every three days! It has been proved that 102 of these were the work of known fascists! There are serious indications that of the remaining 71 over half are attributable to fascists or extreme right para-military groups! Would you agree with those figures Superintendent?

SUPERINTENDENT: They sound a little exaggerated...

FELETTI: But basically correct?

SUPERINTENDENT: Maybe.

PISSANI: We can have them checked out.

FELETTI: And while you are at it kindly check to see how many of these disgusting incidents were mounted in such a way as to point suspicion to the left.

MANIAC: What are you hoping to achieve by these provocative tactics Miss Feletti?

PISSANI: Viper.

MANIAC: Are you trying to get us to admit that instead of chasing idiotic anarchists and relying on informers and agents inside the revolutionary left, we should be concentrating our efforts on para-military fascist organisations trained and supported by, say, the *Greek junta*! and financed by top industrialists both *here and in Spain*!?

SUPERINTENDENT's *eyes are popping.* BERTOZZO *is going nuts.*

PISSANI: Don't worry. It's just his technique – Jesuit dialectics.

MANIAC: Are you suggesting we should turn our attention to those elements in our society who stand to gain by these outrages?

SUPERINTENDENT: Has he gone mad?

BERTOZZO: Mad?

MANIAC: Expose the links between fascist politicians like those in the *M.S.I.*! and government ministers? Even turn the spotlight on *senior officers in the police force itself*?!!

BERTOZZO: Mad.

MANIAC: If you are, then we'd certainly bring some real pus to the surface.

BERTOZZO *is circling the* MANIAC *looking at him from all angles as if he were an exhibit.*

SUPERINTENDENT: Jesuit dialectics?

MANIAC: That's right. I think you are absolutely correct, Miss Feletti.

SUPERINTENDENT: What?

FELETTI: (*To audience*) Well I'm completely disconcerted to hear such statements from a policeman.

BERTOZZO *discovers his hat and coat on coat stand.*

BERTOZZO: Mad.

The light dawns.

BERTOZZO: Mad!! It's him!! It's that fucking maniac! It's him! (*To* SUPERINTENDENT) Sir, I've realised who he is.

SUPERINTENDENT: Well keep it to yourself.

MANIAC *and* FELETTI *are in deep conversation.*

BERTOZZO: (*To* PISSANI) I know who he is! He's in disguise!

PISSANI: So what's new?

BERTOZZO: He's a madman!

SUPERINTENDENT: You are a madman. Will you shut up?!

BERTOZZO: I won't shut up!

They jump on BERTOZZO, *covering his mouth. While* BERTOZZO, CONSTABLE, SUPERINTENDENT *and* PISSANI *are wrestling on the floor the* MANIAC *continues, oblivious.*

MANIAC: You are a journalist Miss Feletti, so you want to use your pen to lance the public boil; but what will you achieve? A huge scandal, a heap of big nobs compromised, head of the police force shunted off into retirement.

FELETTI: Not a bad day's work.

MANIAC: It's just another chance for the pristine beauticians of the Communist Party to point out another wart on the body politic and pose themselves as the party of honesty. But the STATE, Miss Feletti, the State remains, still presenting corruption as the exception to the rule, when the system the State was designed to protect is corruption itself. Corruption *is* the rule.

BERTOZZO: I'll show you.

BERTOZZO *escapes from the melée and dashes across to* MANIAC. *Snatches off his eye patch.*

BERTOZZO: Look! See! He's got an eye! Fuck it!

SUPERINTENDENT: Course he's got a fucking eye!

BERTOZZO: He's got two!

PISSANI: It's the normal number, isn't it?

BERTOZZO: Why was he wearing an eye patch if he's got a bloody eye then?

MANIAC: For amusement.

PISSANI: There you are!

SUPERINTENDENT: For amusement, see.

SUPERINTENDENT: ⎫ Ha! Ha! Ha!
PISSANI: ⎭

BERTOZZO: He's not Pi... !!

They launch themselves at BERTOZZO. *He falls to the ground. They all end up on the ground. They chase him off through the door.*

MANIAC: Where were we?

FELETTI: Scandal.

MANIAC: Ah yes. The people want truth so offer them scandal. The people want jobs, houses and health; the economic system can't provide, so offer reforms before the people chuck the system out and start looking for a better one.

FELETTI: All very true. In the meantime what are you proposing? We do nothing? I collaborate with this cover-up?

MANIAC: Of course not. Expose away. But show how this is not an isolated pocket of wickedness here.

BERTOZZO *enters. Sees* MANIAC. MANIAC *points through the other door.*

MANIAC: That way!

BERTOZZO: (*On his way out*) Sorry.

MANIAC: That's alright.

BERTOZZO *exits.*

MANIAC: Corruption is inevitable under a system of society

which only survives through the exploitation of one class by
another.

SUPERINTENDENT *and* PISSANI *enter chasing*
BERTOZZO.

MANIAC: That way!

PISSANI: Sorry.

MANIAC: That's alright.

SUPERINTENDENT *and* PISSANI *exit.*

MANIAC: Show how these gruesome excesses reflect the
cynicism of the State. (*Starts to remove his wooden leg*)
Don't strengthen the system by providing the State with a
ready-made chance to simply improve its window-dressing.

FELETTI: Just exactly who are you?

BERTOZZO *enters.*

BERTOZZO: Exactly!

Enter SUPERINTENDENT *and* PISSANI.

BERTOZZO: Look, it's his leg! It's false.

PISSANI: Of course it's false!

SUPERINTENDENT: It's a false leg.

BERTOZZO: It's a *false*, false leg.

MANIAC: It's walnut to be precise.

BERTOZZO: He had it strapped to his knee!

FELETTI: What's going on?

SUPERINTENDENT: I do apologise Miss Feletti, but the
Inspector's mordant epilepsy appears to have taken a turn
for the worse.

BERTOZZO: I'm not epileptic! That man is an imposter. He
is not...

SUPERINTENDENT:
PISSANI: } Oggy, oggy, oggy, oi, oi, oi!

SUPERINTENDENT *and* PISSANI *make a leap for*

BERTOZZO. *He escapes. Grabs* CONSTABLE's *revolver from its holster.*

BERTOZZO: Hands up! Backs to the wall or I fire!

PISSANI: What the heck!

BERTOZZO: I said hands up! EVERYONE! I warn you I am no longer responsible!

FELETTI: Oh God!

SUPERINTENDENT: Now then Bertozzo, calm down...

BERTOZZO: You calm down. AGAINST THE FUCKING AUDIENCE (*To audience*) Sorry!

They all go to the front of the stage. BERTOZZO *produces handcuffs. He hands them to* FELETTI.

BERTOZZO: OK, Miss, if you would do the honours. Handcuff them to the window frame.

FELETTI *handcuffs the three policemen to the window frame.*

BERTOZZO: You'll see... you see, sir... I'm sorry... I'm ever so sorry, but this is the only way I can get you to listen to me. Right! (*Turns to* MANIAC) You arsehole! You will do me the honour of telling these people who you really are.

MANIAC: With the greatest pleasure.

PISSANI:
SUPERINTENDENT: } No. Don't do it. You'll destroy it all.
CONSTABLE:

No one has noticed in the confusion that the MANIAC *has been fiddling with the bomb.*

BERTOZZO: Show them the documents. All the records from the psychiatric clinic!

He takes the files from his bag and hands them to the SUPERINTENDENT *who reads incredulously. Passes papers on to* PISSANI.

MANIAC: Fifty years ago the workers of Europe wanted revolution, Miss Feletti. What did they get instead?

Depression, war and a smothering dose of reforms; or rather, an avalanche of promises.

MANIAC *seats himself near the bomb.*

MANIAC: Scandal! People love it! It's like the smell of your own shit!

SUPERINTENDENT: 'Subject to paranoid fits... ?'

PISSANI: Psychiatric hospitals of Imola...

SUPERINTENDENT: ...Voghera...

CONSTABLE: ...Parma...

BERTOZZO: You see.

MANIAC: Take Watergate for instance.

FELETTI: What?

MANIAC: Half the White House on a gangster's payroll, the big cheese pronounced guilty, what happens? He writes a bestseller, meets David Frost, lectures at Oxford and he's laughing all the way to the fucking bank; and Carter promises 'open government'. You see, scandal followed by promises.

FELETTI: What are you on about?

PISSANI: 'Histriomania...'

SUPERINTENDENT: 'Pyromania...'

CONSTABLE: ' ...dipsomania... '

FELETTI: This play was written before Carter was even heard of.

SUPERINTENDENT: He's a lunatic?

BERTOZZO: Exactly.

PISSANI: Him? You mean a mental case came in here, passed himself off as a judge, re-opened the enquiry...

SUPERINTENDENT: Made me sing!

MANIAC: (*Getting carried away. To audience*) How many more Russian spies are downing port at Buckingham Palace? Why did the Anthony Blunt cover-up happen?

Why? Because class runs thicker than nationhood or ideology. But who gives a TINKER'S about that – what the scandal-mongering press care about Blunt is whether he is knocking off Guy Burgess.

SUPERINTENDENT: (*Name of actor who is playing the part*) This isn't Dario Fo.

MANIAC: I know, but I love a bit of political gossip. What about the bastard politicians and businessmen mixed-up in busting Rhodesian oil sanctions? We all know who they are. Are there any arrests? Not fucking likely. Meanwhile innocent black kids can't walk the streets for fear of getting picked up on SUS charges.

PISSANI: This is unheard of distortion of the author's meaning!

MANIAC: He'll get his royalties. Who's moaning?

PISSANI: Get back to the script!

SUPERINTENDENT: This is an insult to Dario Fo!

FELETTI: Good. I've got a bone to pick with him. Why is there only one woman's part in his blasted play? I feel marooned!

MANIAC: The author's sexist?

FELETTI: He's pre-historic!

BERTOZZO: Then why are we bothering?

MANIAC: He's a pre-historic genius! On with the dance!

PISSANI: You mean a mental case came in here, passed himself off as a judge, re-opened the enquiry...

SUPERINTENDENT: Made me sing!

BERTOZZO: Yes. He's a nut. A maniac.

SUPERINTENDENT: When I think of what he put me through...

MANIAC: Nothing to what I'm going to put you through now!

MANIAC produces tape recorder and switches it on.

BERTOZZO: What?

Tape recording. Voices from page 46.

SUPERINTENDENT: You didn't enjoy yourself of course?!

PISSANI: I was having a laugh. Yes. You said that, didn't you, Constable!

CONSTABLE: Yes.

SUPERINTENDENT: Some laugh! Ha! Laughing now, aren't we?!

PISSANI: I was just scaring him. *You* are the nutter!

SUPERINTENDENT: I'm a nutter?!

CONSTABLE: Please!

PISSANI: Well you bloody pushed him, chum!

SUPERINTENDENT: Did I? Did I? That is a laugh alright! All on my own, was I?

FELETTI *is transfixed by the tape. As it plays, the* MANIAC *divests himself of his disguises.*

MANIAC: Everything is on there. Everything you said since I first came in.

FELETTI *turns to see* MANIAC. *Intake of breath.*

FELETTI: You!

BERTOZZO: You know him?

FELETTI: Yes. Paulo Davidovitch Gandolpho.

THE FOUR POLICEMEN: No!!

FELETTI: Prose Pimpernel of the Permanent Revolution.

THE FOUR POLICEMEN: Ah!

FELETTI: The notorious sports editor of *Lotta Continua*!

SUPERINTENDENT: The organ of the Jewish conspiracy itself!

MANIAC: The 'lunatic' fringe. Get it?

SUPERINTENDENT: Get the gun, Bertozzo! Use the gun! Kill him!

MANIAC *produces the bomb. His hand is inside it.*

MANIAC: I wouldn't.

FELETTI: My God, no.

SUPERINTENDENT: Don't be fooled, Bertozzo. It can't go off.

MANIAC: I only need half a finger to flick the detonator.

BERTOZZO: There is no detonator.

MANIAC: Want a bet?

BERTOZZO *approaches.* MANIAC *holds up the bomb.*

BERTOZZO: (*Nearly fainting*) A longbar acoustic...

PISSANI: Not a...

SUPERINTENDENT: ...longbar...

CONSTABLE: ...acoustic?

BERTOZZO: Yes. Where did that come from?

MANIAC: I always keep a few knick-knacks handy. Drop the gun on the desk.

BERTOZZO *does so.*

MANIAC: Join your colleagues.

BERTOZZO *handcuffs himself to the window frame.*

SUPERINTENDENT: What do you intend to do with that tape?

MANIAC: Make a few hundred copies. Spread them around. Plenty of scandal, Miss Feletti, you should be pleased. You lot won't be around to see it, of course.

PISSANI: What do you mean?

MANIAC: Even if I managed a ten minute start on you, every copper in Milan would have orders to shoot me on sight in fifteen. The keys, Miss Feletti. Both of them. No I need to get this lot published and on the streets, that'll take a day and a half at least.

FELETTI *collects both sets of handcuff keys. Puts them on*

desk. MANIAC *picks up bomb.*

SUPERINTENDENT: What are you doing?

MANIAC: This bomb will explode in five minutes precisely.

PISSANI: NO!

MANIAC: Yes.

CONSTABLE: Help!

SUPERINTENDENT: You're a madman.

MANIAC: No comment.

FELETTI: You can't intend to commit slaughter in cold blood?

MANIAC: Why ever not? You think *they* wouldn't? Haven't even? Look at them, the children of Hitler and Mussolini. Same breed as the Pinochets of today.

FELETTI: You can't take the law into your own hands?

MANIAC: Listen. I don't have much choice. Any other course of action and I'll be pushing up the daisies for definite.

FELETTI: Justice must be administered openly through the courts.

SUPERINTENDENT: Here here!

PISSANI: I agree.

MANIAC: It's a nice idea but I haven't got time to mess...

FELETTI: You kill them and you are no better than they are. You merely demonstrate your ultra-left contempt for democracy!

MANIAC: What?

SUPERINTENDENT: Well said, Miss Feletti.

CONSTABLE: Help!

MANIAC: While you Communist Party journalists pass yourselves off as champions of truth and peddle your reformist illusions in the capitalist press I'm supposed to defend democracy by volunteering for the mortuary slab!

Why not ask yourself, Miss Feletti, what sort of democracy requires the services of dogs such as these? I'll tell you. Bourgeois democracy which wears a thin skin of human rights to keep out the cold, but when things hot up, when the rotten plots of the ruling class fail to silence our demands, when they have put half the population on the dole queue and squeezed the other half dry with wage cuts to keep themselves in profit, when they have run out of promises and you reformists have failed to keep the masses in order for them; well *then* they shed their skins and dump you, as they did in Chile; and set their wildest dogs loose on us all.

SUPERINTENDENT: What's going on?

PISSANI: Are you both crazy? There's only three minutes left and you start having a political debate.

CONSTABLE: Help!

SUPERINTENDENT: Miss Feletti!

FELETTI: What has the tragedy in Chile to do with all this?

MANIAC: It's the purest example so far of the failure of the peaceful road to socialism.

CONSTABLE: Oh fucking hell!

MANIAC: That absurd notion which says bourgeois democracy can be gradually transformed from within; that the workers can achieve their liberation without the complete destruction of the capitalist State.

FELETTI: Rubbish.

PISSANI: Two minutes.

CONSTABLE: Help!

FELETTI: Allende's failure proves exactly the opposite. He tried to force the pace of the revolution before the people were fully prepared. He moved too fast.

SUPERINTENDENT: For God's sake!

BERTOZZO: Mercy!

MANIAC: You mean he disarmed the workers too fast, and led them like the Pied Piper into Santiago Stadium. Look at them! The political police armed against the people! Do you seriously imagine you can disarm them with the ballot box? What the hell do you think they are there for? These four were there torturing students at the CRS HQ in Paris in May '68, in the USA at Attica, at Kent State. (*Gives detailed examples of political murder and state repression in Britain*) All this in the name of 'justice' and 'democracy'.

SUPERINTENDENT: } HELP!
PISSANI:

CONSTABLE: } HELP!
BERTOZZO:

FELETTI: You are an extremist! A hooligan! A fanatic! I shan't allow you to go through with this outrage.

MANIAC: You can't stop me.

FELETTI: OK, kill me too or I'll expose the whole thing. (*She blocks the doorway*)

BERTOZZO: Bravo!

MANIAC: Yes, you're good at that.

FELETTI: You will be hunted throughout Europe.

PISSANI: One minute!

FELETTI: Have you the stomach for that?

MANIAC: Certainly. Here. Have you the stomach for this? There's the keys to the handcuffs. I'm off. You can't chuck the bomb out of the window, it's a public street. So... Release them, write your story, but the evidence will die with me and this bunch will undoubtedly be acquitted. Don't release them and you become my accomplice – you join the ranks of the extremists. It's all yours.

Gives her keys to handcuffs. Exit MANIAC. FELETTI stands rigid with indecision.

BERTOZZO: Quick! Quick! Miss Feletti, the keys!

SUPERINTENDENT: Please, Miss Feletti!

PISSANI: I'll face trial, anything!

CONSTABLE: Help!

ALL: Help! HELP! HELP!

MANIAC *appears round the set. Talks to audience.*

MANIAC: She has to decide, you see. I mean, be fair. Some questions just can't be resolved gradually. Especially when you've only get thirty seconds left. Let's see what she decides.

FELETTI *decides. A look of resolution. She looks at the* FOUR POLICEMEN. *Turns and bolts for the door.*

ALL: HELP!

MANIAC: Bravo!

THE FOUR: HELP! HELP!

MANIAC: (*Waves to* POLICEMEN *just before explosion*) Bye!

A massive explosion. Lights. Blackout. Spot on MANIAC.

MANIAC: That's what I call a happy ending!

False exit.

MANIAC: However the drama critics won't go along with that – I mean we can't have the ultra-left hooligan winning hands down like that. Surely a good reformist like Maria Feletti must ensure that decency and the rule of law prevails. So let's see that version.

Lights up. Four handcuffed. FELETTI *undecided. She decides. Rushes to the policemen and starts to unlock handcuffs.*

ALL: HELP!

CONSTABLE: Bless you! Bless you!

PISSANI: I'll pray for you every day of my life.

SUPERINTENDENT: You're an angel. An angel of mercy.

BERTOZZO: Save me! Save me!

All free they rush for the door. Suddenly stop.

SUPERINTENDENT: She knows! She knows everything!

BERTOZZO: QUICK!

They grab FELETTI *and handcuff her to the window frame.*

FELETTI: No! You murderers! Help!

PISSANI: Quick! Run for it!

They all exit fast, laughing.

FELETTI: HELP! HELP!

Blackout except for spot.

MANIAC: Oh *Dio*! Whichever way it goes, you see, you've got to decide. Goodnight.

Postscript

In this Postscript written for the 1974 Einaudi edition of
Accidental Death of an Anarchist, *Dario Fo describes the
genesis of the play and its impact in Italy. The translation is by
Ed Emery.*

How did we hit upon the idea of staging a show based on the
theme of the State massacre? Here, we were driven once
again by force of circumstances. During the Spring of 1970 the
comrades who were coming to see our shows – workers,
students and progressives – were asking us to write a
full-length piece on the Milan bombings and the murder of
Pinelli, a piece which would discuss the political motives and
consequences of these events. The reason for their request
was the terrible shortage of information on the subject. Once
the Press had got over the initial shock, they went silent. The
newspapers of the official Left parties – with *L'Unità* at their
head – refused to take sides, and limited themselves to the odd
comment such as: 'This is a worrying episode', or 'The
circumstances surrounding both Pinelli's death and the
massacres at the banks are obscure and shrouded in mystery.'
They had decided to wait for 'light to be shed' – waiting, so as
to avoid making too much fuss.

But no. This was precisely the time to make a fuss, with
every means available: so that people who are always thinking
about other things, who don't read much and don't read well,
and even then are only interested in their own patch, could be
told how the State is capable of organising a massacre and at
the same time organise the mourning, the public outrage, the

medals for the widows and orphans, and the official funerals with carabinieri presenting arms and standing to attention.

At the begining of that Summer, Samonà-Savelli had published the book *La Strage di Stato* (published as 'Italian State Massacre', Libertaria, London, 1971): this was an extraordinarily detailed documentation, packed with material, which showed great courage and determination on the part of its authors. Then, in the Autumn, legal proceedings were started by Inspector Calabresi against the newspaper *Lotta Continua*, and its editor Pio Baldelli. It was at this point that we too realised that it was time to get something moving as soon as possible.

We in turn embarked on a research project. A group of lawyers and journalists made available to us photocopies of several articles which had been prepared by democratic and left-wing newspapers but never published. We were also lucky enough to get our hands on various documents from the court proceedings, as well as being able to read the judges' Order for the Pinelli case to be shelved (and, as we know, the important trials which, in some people's view, would have 'shed light' on the episode, were subsequently postponed and then abandoned definitively: by reason of the non-accidental death of the actor).[1]

We drew up a first draft of the play. It was, naturally, a farce, because such was the painful grotesqueness of the court proceedings and the contradictions in official statements. We were informed that we might be running the risk of legal proceedings, with trials and charges being brought against us. Nevertheless, we decided not only that it was worth the effort to try, but also that it was our duty as political militants. The important thing was to act and to act fast.

The first night of the play, in our converted warehouse theatre in via Colletta, coincided with the trial of Pio Baldelli. It was an extraordinary popular success: every evening the theatre was sold out half an hour before the performance began, and we ended up performing with people on the stage, in the wings. Despite the provocations: the usual phone calls from unnamed callers telling us that there was a bomb in the theatre; the interventions of the Flying Squad; the way the bosses' Press highlighted the incident; despite all this, we were encouraged to hold firm by the lawyer comrades in the Calabresi-Baldelli case, and performances continued, with full houses, away past mid-January.

Our difficulties began when we set off on tour. In via Colletta [2] we were on home ground. Outside Milan, the comrades who were organising things for us went out to try and hire theatres, cinemas and dance halls. There was more than one hall-owner who refused to let us use his premises, even though we were prepared to pay for any damage, since somebody had had a quiet word with him. Somebody who didn't want to lose his job as local police chief.

Often, though, apparent defeats were turned into victories. At Bologna, for example, we were denied the use of the 1,500-seat Duse Theatre. But instead we managed to get the 6,000 seats of the Sports Stadium, and the people came and packed it. It began to become clear that the police and one or two mayors more or less in league with the government, were making an effort to prevent certain things being known about... Well, certain things absolutely *had* to be known about.

But what has been the real reason for the show's success? It is not so much the way it mocks the hypocrisies, the lies that are organised so grossly and blatantly (which is putting it mildly) by the constituted organs of the State and by the functionaries who serve them (judges, police chiefs, prefects, undersecretaries and ministers); it has been above all the way it deals with social democracy and its crocodile tears, the indignation which can be relieved by a little burp in the form of scandal; scandal as a liberating catharsis of the system. A burp which liberates itself precisely through the scandal that explodes, when it is discovered that massacres, giant frauds and murders are undertaken by the organs of power, but that at the same time, from within the powers-that-be, other organs, perhaps pushed by an enraged public opinion, denounce them and unmask them. The indignation of the good democratic citizen grows and threatens to suffocate him. But he has a sense of satisfaction when he sees, in the end, these same organs of this rotten and corrupt society, pointing the finger at this selfsame society, at its own 'unhealthy parts', and this gives him a sense of freedom throughout his whole being. With his spirit suitably decongested, he shouts: 'Long live this bastard shit society, because at least it always wipes its bum with soft, perfumed paper, and when it burps it has the good manners to put its hand in front of its mouth!'

Accidental Death of an Anarchist has been running for two seasons now. It has been performed something like 300 times, and has been seen by more than 300,000 people. In the meantime, the spiral of the strategy of tension has increased, and has created other victims: the play has been brought up to date, and its message has been made more explicit. With the death of Feltrinelli, [3] a long introductory section was added, and the title was changed to *Morte accidentale di un anarchico e di alcuni altri sovversivi* ('Accidental death of an anarchist, and of other subversives'). Our immediate intention was to make it clear that the State massacre is continuing relentlessly, and that it remains motivated by the same people. The same people who have kept Valpreda and his comrades in prison in the hope that they will die; the same people who have beaten a young man in the streets of Pisa and then in prison and finally killed him; the same ones who are behind a revolutionary militant getting stabbed in Parma – not just an 'anti-fascist youth', as the revisionists are claiming. The same people who are preparing for an Autumn of reaction and violence, preceding it with blackmail against the movement, against all those who are not willing to bow their heads.

But unluckily for them, they will have to realise that there are a lot of us... and that this time their burp is going to stick in their throats.

For the La Comune Theatre Collective
DARIO FO

[1] Inspector Calabresi – high-ranking police officer central to the Pinelli affair and possibly Inspector Defenestration himself. Sued the left-wing paper *Lotta Continua* for defamation. Shortly after was assassinated – hence the reference to the non-accidental death of the actor.

[2] Via Colletta – the warehouse in Milan occupied by the La Comune

theatre collective, which was the base for their militant theatrical activities.

[3] Feltrinelli – head of the influential left-wing publishing house of that name, which published many of the major left-wing and revolutionary texts of this period. Found in extremely suspicious circumstances with explosive materials near a power pylon. His death has never been explained.

Bloomsbury Methuen Drama Modern Plays

include work by

Bola Agbaje
Edward Albee
Davey Anderson
Jean Anouilh
John Arden
Peter Barnes
Sebastian Barry
Alistair Beaton
Brendan Behan
Edward Bond
William Boyd
Bertolt Brecht
Howard Brenton
Amelia Bullmore
Anthony Burgess
Leo Butler
Jim Cartwright
Lolita Chakrabarti
Caryl Churchill
Lucinda Coxon
Curious Directive
Nick Darke
Shelagh Delaney
Ishy Din
Claire Dowie
David Edgar
David Eldridge
Dario Fo
Michael Frayn
John Godber
Paul Godfrey
James Graham
David Greig
John Guare
Mark Haddon
Peter Handke
David Harrower
Jonathan Harvey
Iain Heggie

Robert Holman
Caroline Horton
Terry Johnson
Sarah Kane
Barrie Keeffe
Doug Lucie
Anders Lustgarten
David Mamet
Patrick Marber
Martin McDonagh
Arthur Miller
D. C. Moore
Tom Murphy
Phyllis Nagy
Anthony Neilson
Peter Nichols
Joe Orton
Joe Penhall
Luigi Pirandello
Stephen Poliakoff
Lucy Prebble
Peter Quilter
Mark Ravenhill
Philip Ridley
Willy Russell
Jean-Paul Sartre
Sam Shepard
Martin Sherman
Wole Soyinka
Simon Stephens
Peter Straughan
Kate Tempest
Theatre Workshop
Judy Upton
Timberlake Wertenbaker
Roy Williams
Snoo Wilson
Frances Ya-Chu Cowhig
Benjamin Zephaniah

Bloomsbury Methuen Drama Student Editions

Jean Anouilh *Antigone* • John Arden *Serjeant Musgrave's Dance* • Alan Ayckbourn *Confusions* • Aphra Behn *The Rover* • Edward Bond *Lear* • *Saved* • Bertolt Brecht *The Caucasian Chalk Circle* • *Fear and Misery in the Third Reich* • *The Good Person of Szechwan* • *Life of Galileo* • *Mother Courage and Her Children* • *The Resistible Rise of Arturo Ui* • *The Threepenny Opera* • Anton Chekhov *The Cherry Orchard* • *The Seagull* • *Three Sisters* • *Uncle Vanya* • Caryl Churchill *Serious Money* • *Top Girls* • Shelagh Delaney *A Taste of Honey* • Euripides *Elektra* • *Medea* • Dario Fo *Accidental Death of an Anarchist* • Michael Frayn *Copenhagen* • John Galsworthy *Strife* • Nikolai Gogol *The Government Inspector* • Carlo Goldoni *A Servant to Two Masters* • Lorraine Hansberry *A Raisin in the Sun* • Robert Holman *Across Oka* • Henrik Ibsen *A Doll's House* • *Ghosts* • *Hedda Gabler* • Sarah Kane *4.48 Psychosis* • *Blasted* • Charlotte Keatley *My Mother Said I Never Should* • Bernard Kops *Dreams of Anne Frank* • Federico García Lorca *Blood Wedding* • *Doña Rosita the Spinster* (bilingual edition) • *The House of Bernarda Alba* (bilingual edition) • *Yerma* (bilingual edition) • David Mamet *Glengarry Glen Ross* • *Oleanna* • Patrick Marber *Closer* • John Marston *The Malcontent* • Martin McDonagh *The Lieutenant of Inishmore* • *The Lonesome West* • *The Beauty Queen of Leenane* • Arthur Miller *All My Sons* • *The Crucible* • *A View from the Bridge* • *Death of a Salesman* • *The Price* • *After the Fall* • *The Last Yankee* • *A Memory of Two Mondays* • *Broken Glass* • Joe Orton *Loot* • Joe Penhall *Blue/Orange* • Luigi Pirandello *Six Characters in Search of an Author* • Lucy Prebble *Enron* • Mark Ravenhill *Shopping and F***ing* • Willy Russell *Blood Brothers* • *Educating Rita* • Sophocles *Antigone* • *Oedipus the King* • Wole Soyinka *Death and the King's Horseman* • Shelagh Stephenson *The Memory of Water* • August Strindberg *Miss Julie* • J. M. Synge *The Playboy of the Western World* • Theatre Workshop *Oh What a Lovely War* • Frank Wedekind *Spring Awakening* • Timberlake Wertenbaker *Our Country's Good* • Arnold Wesker *The Merchant* • Oscar Wilde *The Importance of Being Earnest* • Tennessee Williams *A Streetcar Named Desire* • *The Glass Menagerie* • *Cat on a Hot Tin Roof* • *Sweet Bird of Youth*

Bloomsbury Methuen Drama World Classics
include

Jean Anouilh (two volumes)
John Arden (two volumes)
Brendan Behan
Aphra Behn
Bertolt Brecht (eight volumes)
Georg Büchner
Mikhail Bulgakov
Pedro Calderón
Karel Čapek
Peter Nichols (two volumes)
Anton Chekhov
Noël Coward (eight volumes)
Georges Feydeau (two volumes)
Eduardo De Filippo
Max Frisch (two volumes)
John Galsworthy
Nikolai Gogol (two volumes)
Maxim Gorky (two volumes)
Harley Granville Barker
(two volumes)
Victor Hugo
Henrik Ibsen (six volumes)

Alfred Jarry
Federico García Lorca
(three volumes)
Pierre Marivaux
Mustapha Matura
David Mercer
(two volumes)
Arthur Miller (six volumes)
Molière
Pierre de Musset
Joe Orton
A. W. Pinero
Luigi Pirandello
Terence Rattigan
W. Somerset Maugham
August Strindberg
(three volumes)
J. M. Synge
Ramón del Valle-Inclán
Frank Wedekind
Oscar Wilde
Tennessee Williams

Bloomsbury Methuen Drama Contemporary Dramatists

include

John Arden (two volumes)
Arden & D'Arcy
Peter Barnes (three volumes)
Sebastian Barry
Mike Bartlett
Dermot Bolger
Edward Bond (eight volumes)
Howard Brenton (two volumes)
Leo Butler
Richard Cameron
Jim Cartwright
Caryl Churchill (two volumes)
Complicite
Sarah Daniels (two volumes)
Nick Darke
David Edgar (three volumes)
David Eldridge (two volumes)
Ben Elton
Per Olov Enquist
Dario Fo (two volumes)
Michael Frayn (four volumes)
John Godber (four volumes)
Paul Godfrey
James Graham
David Greig
John Guare
Lee Hall (two volumes)
Katori Hall
Peter Handke
Jonathan Harvey (two volumes)
Iain Heggie
Israel Horovitz
Declan Hughes
Terry Johnson (three volumes)
Sarah Kane
Barrie Keeffe
Bernard-Marie Koltès (two volumes)
Franz Xaver Kroetz
Kwame Kwei-Armah
David Lan
Bryony Lavery
Deborah Levy
Doug Lucie

David Mamet (four volumes)
Patrick Marber
Martin McDonagh
Duncan McLean
David Mercer (two volumes)
Anthony Minghella (two volumes)
Tom Murphy (six volumes)
Phyllis Nagy
Anthony Neilson (two volumes)
Peter Nichol (two volumes)
Philip Osment
Gary Owen
Louise Page
Stewart Parker (two volumes)
Joe Penhall (two volumes)
Stephen Poliakoff (three volumes)
David Rabe (two volumes)
Mark Ravenhill (three volumes)
Christina Reid
Philip Ridley (two volumes)
Willy Russell
Eric-Emmanuel Schmitt
Ntozake Shange
Sam Shepard (two volumes)
Martin Sherman (two volumes)
Christopher Shinn
Joshua Sobel
Wole Soyinka (two volumes)
Simon Stephens (three volumes)
Shelagh Stephenson
David Storey (three volumes)
C. P. Taylor
Sue Townsend
Judy Upton
Michel Vinaver (two volumes)
Arnold Wesker (two volumes)
Peter Whelan
Michael Wilcox
Roy Williams (four volumes)
David Williamson
Snoo Wilson (two volumes)
David Wood (two volumes)
Victoria Wood

Bloomsbury Methuen Drama
Classical Greek Dramatists

Aeschylus Plays: One
(Persians, Seven Against Thebes, Suppliants,
Prometheus Bound)

Aeschylus Plays: Two
(Oresteia: Agamemnon, Libation-Bearers, Eumenides)

Aristophanes Plays: One
(Acharnians, Knights, Peace, Lysistrata)

Aristophanes Plays: Two
(Wasps, Clouds, Birds, Festival Time, Frogs)

Aristophanes & Menander: New Comedy
(Women in Power, Wealth, The Malcontent,
The Woman from Samos)

Euripides Plays: One
(Medea, The Phoenician Women, Bacchae)

Euripides Plays: Two
(Hecuba, The Women of Troy, Iphigeneia at Aulis, Cyclops)

Euripides Plays: Three
(Alkestis, Helen, Ion)

Euripides Plays: Four
(Elektra, Orestes, Iphigeneia in Tauris)

Euripides Plays: Five
(Andromache, Herakles' Children, Herakles)

Euripides Plays: Six
(Hippolytos, Suppliants, Rhesos)

Sophocles Plays: One
(Oedipus the King, Oedipus at Colonus, Antigone)

Sophocles Plays: Two
(Ajax, Women of Trachis, Electra, Philoctetes)

For a complete listing of Bloomsbury
Methuen Drama titles, visit:

www.bloomsbury.com/drama

Follow us on Twitter and keep up to date
with our news and publications

@MethuenDrama